Bayern von oben
Bavaria from above

PAGES 2/3

Simply the highest

The Alps were the first high mountain range to be systematically measured by researchers. As a result, they gave the term to world vocabulary that refers to the altitude above the tree line: wherever wind, ice and snow blow fiercely without any resistance, it is designated as »alpine«.

SEITEN 2/3

Einfach das Höchste

Die Alpen, das erste Hochgebirge, an dem Forscher systematisch Maß nahmen, gaben dem Welt-Wortschatz eine Bezeichnung für die Höhenstufe über der Baumgrenze: Wo Wind, Eis und Schnee ungebremst angreifen, ist es »alpin«.

PAGES 4/5

A weaving waterway

The Main River almost looks a bit drunk, meandering in narrow curves through Franconia, as it does here, near Muensterschwarzach. But its erratic journey has nothing to do with the vineyards that line the banks of the river valley between Aschaffenburg and Schweinfurt, but rather with the limited possibilities offered to it by the pre-existing geographical formations of Swiss Franconia, the Spessart district, and the Steigerwald and Odenwald forests.

SEITEN 4/5

Torkelnder Verlauf

Fast ein bisschen beschwipst sieht es aus, wie sich der Main in engen Schlaufen durchs Frankenland schlängelt, wie hier bei Münsterschwarzach. Mit den Weinstöcken, die zwischen Aschaffenburg und Schweinfurt an den Talhängen des Mains wachsen, hat dieser torkelnde Verlauf aber nichts zu tun, sondern mit den eingeschränkten Möglichkeiten, die ihm Fränkische Schweiz, Steigerwald, Spessart und Odenwald noch gelassen haben.

PAGES 6/7

Soul searching

It is said that a Benedictine convent once stood near the small Chapel of St. Bartholomew, not far from Kelheim. Apparently its inhabitants broke with the faith and fled the convent's walls. But perhaps not far enough away! According to legend, their souls still flit like will-o'-the-wisps around the nearby lake and chapel, unredeemed and wracked with guilt.

SEITEN 6/7

Seelen im Suchflug

In der Nachbarschaft der kleinen St. Bartholomä-Kapelle, unweit von Kelheim, soll ein Benediktinerinnen-Kloster gestanden haben, dessen Bewohnerinnen vom Glauben abfielen und flohen. Aber vielleicht nicht weit genug! Der Sage nach irrlichtern ihre Seelen immer noch schuldbewusst und unerlöst um den nahen See und die Kapelle.

PAGE 9

Half-timber everywhere

With justified pride, Koenigsberg in Lower Franconia calls itself »Bavaria's Half-timbered Town«. In many cities, this style of building has barely survived – existing only as a nostalgic remnant of the past, squeezed in-between the flat, faceless facades of the modern cityscape. Due to its protected status, however, this architectural style can still be found in abundance in the city of Koenigsberg where it has been placed under historical protection.

SEITE 9

Alles Fachwerk

»Bayerns Fachwerkstadt« nennt sich das unterfränkische Königsberg voll berechtigtem Stolz. Was sich mancherorts nur als wehmütig stimmendes Einsprengsel zwischen den glatten, gesichtslosen Fassaden der modernen Stadtlandschaft erhalten hat, findet sich hier noch als komplettes denkmalgeschütztes Ensemble.

Gerhard Launer
Bayern von oben
Bavaria from above

Mit Texten von
Text by Gernot Geurtzen

*Translated from
the German by* Sascha Hastings

KNESEBECK

A View over Bavaria

An old Bavarian saying is inscribed on the wall of Esting Castle's chapel for all to read: »Extra Bavariam nulla vita, et si est vita, non est ita!« It translates as »Outside Bavaria, there is no life, and even if there is, it is certainly not this one!« Immediately, the image springs to mind of a Bavarian, gazing out over the landscape. Naturally he enjoys a lofty vantage point high up a hill, on a bench in front of his front door, or perhaps in the sun of the beer garden at the monastery of Andechs. As he takes in the splendidly idyllic scenery of the Lower Alps, he is so utterly content with himself and the world, so completely at peace, that he considers himself to be chosen or blessed. He cannot imagine any reason why he would ever want to leave this place. No-one need explain to him why so many non-Bavarians want to come here.

Bavarians have no need for modesty. Bavaria is not simply the largest German province, equal to the combined size of the Netherlands and Belgium, it is also the most popular holiday destination in Germany and the province which boasts the highest quality of living. Bavaria has the grandest mountains in the entire country, some of its most picturesque lakes, and a wealth of impressive cultural monuments, which make it famous throughout the world – so famous, in fact, that people often confuse Bavaria with the entire German state and, from Japan to Texas, first think of the Alps, Neuschwanstein Castle, Oktoberfest, and brass-band music when they hear the word »Germany«.

The corollary of this enviable international reputation is that it can be hard to look at Bavaria without having your vision blurred by clichés or stereotypes. Indeed, there are many of these, both in and outside Germany: for example, the Bavarian as King Ludwig fan, with a tuft of chamois hair in his hat and an Edelweiss flower tucked into his buttonhole, spending all his free time doing the local high-hopping, knee-slapping folk dance. Or, to take a more current stereotype, the Bavarian as someone equally familiar with laptops and Lederhosen. Bava-

Blick auf Bayern

»Extra Bavariam nulla vita, et si est vita, non est ita!« heißt ein alter Spruch in Bayern, zu lesen als Inschrift an der Schlosskapelle Esting: »Außerhalb von Bayern gibt's kein Leben, und wenn doch, dann bestimmt nicht so eins.« Sofort entsteht vor dem inneren Auge das Bild eines Bayern, der, natürlich von einer erhöhten Warte auf einem Hügel aus, auf der Bank vor seiner Haustür, vielleicht auch im Biergarten von Kloster Andechs in der Sonne sitzt, übers Land schaut und angesichts der prächtigen voralpenländischen Idylle mit sich selbst und der Welt zufrieden und im Reinen ist, ja sich irgendwie auserwählt, begnadet fühlt. Warum er jemals von hier weggehen sollte, dafür könnte er sich keinen Grund vorstellen. Warum so viele Nichtbayern ausgerechnet hierher wollen, das muss ihm niemand erklären.

Für Bescheidenheit haben die Bayern auch gar keinen Grund: Bayern ist nicht nur das größte Bundesland, so groß wie die Niederlande und Belgien zusammen, es ist auch das mit Abstand beliebteste Urlaubsziel in Deutschland und gilt als das Bundesland mit der höchsten Lebensqualität. Es hat die mächtigsten Berge Deutschlands, einige der malerischsten Seen und eine Fülle eindrucksvoller Kulturdenkmäler, wofür es in aller Welt berühmt ist. So berühmt, dass Bayern oft sogar mit dem ganzen deutschen Staat gleichgesetzt wird und man von Japan bis Texas beim Stichwort Deutschland zuallererst an die Alpen, Neuschwanstein, Oktoberfest und Blasmusik denkt.

Schon nach zwei Absätzen wird klar: Es ist kaum möglich, einen Blick auf Bayern zu werfen, ohne dass dieser von Klischees getrübt wird. Und deren gibt es viele, außerhalb wie innerhalb Deutschlands: der Bayer als König-Ludwig-Fan, der am Hut den Gamsbart und im Knopfloch das Edelweiß trägt, seine Freizeit mit Schuhplatteln verbringt und neuerdings auch noch mit Laptop und Lederhose gleichermaßen vertraut ist. Bayern – eine barocke Landschaft, in der barocke Menschen unter einem barocken Himmel leben?

ria – is it simply a baroque landscape inhabited by baroque people under a baroque sky?

It is true to say that there is much in Bavaria that is slightly more luxurious than anywhere else: the mountains, the meadows, the clouds, the self-confidence of the people (see above!), the beer mugs, the food, the Bavarian ideal of beauty. Perhaps that is why Bavaria is the only place in the world where the Rococo could actually exceed the Baroque in its sheer opulence, as with the awe-inspiring Wieskirche. Yet, in the same way that the romance origin of the word »baroque« implies the irregular and the out-of-the-ordinary, Bavaria is also a land of contradictions: natural beauty and high tech, loud blasts of the tuba and soft strains of the zither, the avant-garde Blue Rider movement and the historical art of painted facades, postcard-perfect landscapes and the visual monotony of agribusiness, religious piety and zest for living, rebelliousness and subjection to authority, provincialism and openness to the world. Why do the Bavarians have so many different sides to them? Perhaps it is because of the rich variety of their genetic inheritance. When Rome abandoned its province Raetia in the dying days of the Empire 1,500 years ago, the Romans who stayed behind intermarried with local,

centuries-old Celtic peoples and four or five Germanic tribes who had migrated in from the north and east, to create the Bavarian people. A truly homogeneous tribe of »Bajuwaren« never existed, no matter what some past historians have tried to assert.

One could speculate that the cause for everything enigmatic, contradictory or clichéd about the Bavarians lies in the fact that they have always considered themselves a »virtual« people, a people who have had first to find themselves, if not completely invent themselves anew. This may explain the need of Bavarians to constantly reassure themselves of their own identity, as they energetically proclaim their feeling of belonging with the expression »mir san mir« (»we are ourselves«), and always attempt to differentiate themselves from the rest of the world, »extra Bavariam«, in political, social or cultural matters. Above all, they are more bound to tradition than the people of any other province in Germany. In reality, Bavarians are not completely innocent of the fact that these traditions can have elements of the stereotype. For example, Lederhosen are actually an invention of the Romans, who found the climate north of the Alps so unbearable that they wrapped themselves in animal skins,

Der Main/River Main

Tatsächlich ist in Bayern vieles ein bisschen üppiger als anderswo: die Berge, die Wiesen, die Wolken, das Selbstbewusstsein (siehe oben!), die Bierkrüge, das Essen, das Schönheitsideal. Vielleicht konnte deshalb nur hier der Barock an Üppigkeit noch einmal im Rokoko übertroffen werden, wie wir es in der Wieskirche bestaunen können. Doch wie schon im romanischen Ursprung des Wortes »Barock« das Unregelmäßige und Sonderbare steckt, ist Bayern auch ein Land der großen Widersprüche: Naturschönheit und High-Tech, laute Tubatöne und zarte Zitherklänge, Blauer Reiter und Lüftlmalerei, Postkartenlandschaft und flurbereinigte Einöde, Frömmigkeit und Lebenslust, Widerspenstigkeit und Obrigkeitshörigkeit, Provinzialität und Weltoffenheit. Womöglich sind die Bayern ja deshalb so vielseitig, weil sie einem gut durchmischten Genpool entstammen. Denn als vor 1500 Jahren Rom am Ende der Spätantike seine Provinz Raetien räumte, fanden verbleibende Römer, schon seit Jahrhunderten ansässige Kelten und noch vier oder fünf zugewanderte Germanenstämme aus dem Norden und Osten zueinander und verschmolzen zum Volk der Bayern. Einen homogenen Stamm von Bajuwaren, wie es uns einige Historiker früher weismachen wollten, hat es also niemals gegeben.

Fast könnte man vermuten, dass hier die Ursache für all das Rätselhafte, Widersprüchliche und Klischeehafte dieses Volkes liegt: dass es sich nämlich von Anfang an als eine Art virtuelles Volk empfand, das sich erst selbst finden, wenn nicht gar erfinden musste. Vielleicht erklärt sich daher das Bedürfnis der Bayern, sich stets ihrer eigenen Identität zu vergewissern, indem sie mit einem kräftigen »Mir san mir« ihr Zusammengehörigkeitsgefühl beschwören, sich ständig in politischen, gesellschaftlichen oder kulturellen Dingen gegen die Welt »extra Bavariam« abzugrenzen suchen und, vor allem, mehr als jede andere deutsche Völkerschaft den Traditionen verhaftet sind. Dass diese Traditionen manchmal klischeehafte Züge tragen, daran sind die Bayern nicht ganz unschuldig. Die Lederhose zum Beispiel ist in Wahrheit eine Erfindung der Römer, denen das Klima nördlich der Alpen so zu schaffen machte, dass sie sich in Tierfelle mit hosenträgerartigen Riemen verpackten – als Rheumadecke. Später waren lederne Kniehosen eine robuste Arbeitskleidung für Bergbauern und Jäger, bis sie Anfang des 19. Jahrhunderts mit dem europaweiten Siegeszug der langen Hosen fast völlig verschwanden. Erst Ende des Jahrhunderts kam die Lederhose dann wieder in Mode, als reich verzierte Jagd- und

15

Bei Hersbruck/Near Hersbruck

complete with straps that looked like suspenders, to ward off rheumatism. Later, mountain farmers and hunters favoured leather knee-breeches as highly durable working clothes, until they all but disappeared at the beginning of the 19th century that long pants came into vogue across Europe. It was not until the end of that century when Lederhosen came back into fashion, as richly-decorated hunting and holiday clothing for the Bavarian aristocracy. Finally, with the help of newly ubiquitous traditional costume clubs, this formerly humble leg-covering of mountain farmers was modified into what we now know as Lederhosen, and has been a folkloric fashion staple all through Bavaria ever since.

If you are still concerned that you might lose your general overview of this curious and enigmatic province in clichés and contradictions, or if you are seeking a different Bavaria beyond the occasionally operetta-like, or even carnivalesque, beyond the earthy and the robust, the cheerful noise and the garish colours, join Gerhard Launer in a flight across the white-blue skies (admittedly, a final stereotype!), where you'll discover peace, perspective, and a whole new impression of Bavaria. Launer flew over the province in his Cessna, from Lindau to Passau, from the Fichtelgebirge mountains to the Alps, and photographed it all from the air. Through this unusual perspective and his skillful play with light and shadow, sun and cloud, he draws your eye to things you may never have noticed before or offers new ways of seeing what you thought you already knew well.

Twenty years ago, when Gerhard Launer began to combine his two great passions, flying and photography, he encountered a few unexpected difficulties. For one, it proved almost impossible, in full flight, with the control stick in one hand and the remote control shutter release in the other, to steer the plane into exactly the right position and expose the film at the perfect moment, without getting a blurred photographic image. But now, approximately 100,000 photographs later, Launer has overcome his initial problems, not least because he was able to simplify his work with technological innovations which he developed himself. In the early years he half-froze himself by flying with an open side door to give the camera an unobstructed view, later developing a special photo door constructed with an aperture for a built-in lens. In addition, a special spring-suspension underneath the camera insured that it did not shift and thus blur the photographs.

Rosenau

Urlaubskleidung für den bayerischen Adel. Mit Hilfe der damals aus dem Boden sprießenden Trachtenvereine wurde das ehemalige Bergbauernbeinkleid dann als kurze Hose oder als »Bundhose« bayernweit zum kultigen Bestandteil der Folklore.

Wer bei all den Klischees und Widersprüchlichkeiten den Überblick in diesem merkwürdig-rätselhaften Land zu verlieren droht oder wer nach einem anderen Bayern sucht jenseits des manchmal Operettenhaften, ja Karnevalesken, des Deftigen und Kräftigen, des laut Polternden und Grell-Bunten, der begebe sich mit Gerhard Launer hinauf in den weiß-blauen Himmel (um noch ein letztes Klischee zu bemühen) und finde hier Ruhe, Distanz und einen ganz neuen Blick auf dieses Land. Launer hat Bayern mit seiner Cessna überflogen, von Lindau bis Passau, vom Fichtelgebirge bis zu den Alpen, und es aus der Luft fotografiert. Durch die ungewohnte Perspektive und sein gekonntes Spiel mit Licht und Schatten, Sonne und Nebel lenkt er den Blick auf bisher nicht Beachtetes oder eröffnet ganz neue Sichtweisen auf scheinbar Altbekanntes.

Als Gerhard Launer vor zwanzig Jahren damit begann, seine beiden großen Leidenschaften, das Fliegen und das Fotografieren, zu verbinden, stieß er zunächst auf unerwartete Schwierigkeiten: In vollem Flug, den Steuerknüppel in der einen, den Fernauslöser in der anderen Hand, die richtige Position anzusteuern, rechtzeitig abzudrücken und dabei ein unverwackeltes Bild zustande zu bringen, erwies sich fast als ein Ding der Unmöglichkeit. Diese Anfangsprobleme sind nun, rund 100 000 Luftfotografien später, längst überwunden, nicht zuletzt deshalb, weil Launer sich seine Arbeit durch einige selbsterfundene technische Neuerungen erleichtert hat. Während er in den ersten Jahren noch frierend ohne Seitentür geflogen war, damit die Kamera einen ungehinderten Blick hatte, ließ er sich später eine Fototür mit einer Öffnung für die Linse einbauen. Und eine spezielle Federung unter der Kamera verhindert nun, dass die Aufnahmen verwackeln.

Launers Blick auf Bayern ist nicht nur der Blick auf eine besondere Landschaft, sondern zugleich ein Blick zurück in die Vergangenheit. Etwa auf die letzte Eiszeit, in der sich riesige Gletscher von den Alpen herab in die Ebene schoben und die Buckellandschaft des Voralpenraums schufen mit ihren Moränen und ausgeschürften Becken, die sich dann mit Schmelzwasser füllten. So entstanden der Starnberger See und der Ammersee, der Tegern- und der Schliersee und auch das »bayerische Meer«, der Chiemsee. Nur aus der Sicht von oben

Launer's view of Bavaria is not just a look at an exceptional landscape, but also a look back into history – back as far as the last ice age, when giant glaciers swept down from the Alps into the plains below, creating the undulating landscape of the Lower Alps, with its high moraines and scraped out craters that filled with melted water after the glaciers receded. In this way, many of Bavaria's lakes were created, including the Starnbergersee, the Ammersee, the Tegernsee, the Schliersee, and also the »Bavarian Sea«, or Chiemsee. Only from the air can you fully appreciate how, 100 million years ago, the tremendous pressure of the African against the Eurasian tectonic plate began to crumple the earth's crust like a tablecloth, causing the formation of the Alpine range. Another mountain range runs through the middle of Germany; it is three times as old as the Alps, and was once just as massive. But Launer's photographs reveal how the wind and weather gradually eroded all its ridges, peaks and edges over millions of years to create the gently rolling landscapes north of the Danube, including the Mittelgebirge and Fichtelgebirge ranges, the forests of Bavaria, and the Frankischen Alb.

Launer's look at Bavarian rivers is also fascinating. The sky is the best vantage point for witnessing how entire cities sprung up along the banks of rivers: Munich on the Isar, Wuerzburg on the Main, Passau on the Danube. In prehistoric times, these rivers meandered along the path of least resistance, cutting into the landscape and putting their stamp on it, like when the Danube carved a passage through the chalk cliffs separating Kelheim and Wuerzburg. In fact, it is probably thanks to this river, which shaped today's landscape, that this area is one of the most historically significant in Bavaria. Relics of Stone Age peoples and Celts have been found here; the Romans built their fort Abusinia here; and the Limes, a 600 kilometer-long rampart against the Teutonic tribes, stretched westward from this place towards the Rhine. The oldest monastary in Bavaria, Kloster Weltenburg, is also located here, founded around 600 A.D. by itinerant monks from the Vosges mountains. And very close by, enthroned on the peak of the Michelsberg, is the Befreiungshalle or Hall of Liberation, which King Ludwig I built in memory of the Napoleonic Wars – wars that Bavaria fought in, after conveniently switching sides to join Napoleon's enemies shortly before his defeat. This Hall of Liberation appears colossal when you stand directly in front of it, somehow oversized. Only when you view it from

Steingaden

erschließt sich auch, wie sich vor 100 Millionen Jahren durch den Druck der afrikanischen Kontinentalplatte auf die eurasische die Erdkruste wie eine Tischdecke aufzufalten begann und so die Alpenkette entstand. Dreimal so alt ist ein anderer Gebirgszug mitten in Deutschland, einst ebenfalls von alpinen Dimensionen. Wie Wind und Wetter ihn in Jahrmillionen abtrugen und alle Grate, Spitzen und Kanten zu sanften Rundungen abschliffen, das zeigen die Luftaufnahmen von den nördlich der Donau gelegenen Mittelgebirgen, dem Bayerischen und Oberpfälzer Wald, dem Fichtelgebirge und der Fränkischen Alb.

Faszinierend auch Launers Blick auf die bayerischen Flüsse. Von oben erkennt man am besten, wie sich ganze Städte an die Ufer dieser Wasserstraßen anschmiegen, München an die Isar, Würzburg an den Main, Passau an die Donau. Viel früher schon suchten diese Flüsse mäandernd den Weg des geringsten Widerstandes, schnitten sich in die Landschaft ein und drückten ihr ihren Stempel auf, wie es die Donau tat, als sie sich eine Schneise brach durch die Kalkfelsen zwischen Kelheim und Weltenburg. Vermutlich ist es nur dem Fluss, der die Landschaft formte, zu verdanken, dass diese Gegend eine der geschichtsträchtigsten Bayerns

ist: Hier wurden Relikte der Steinzeitmenschen und der Kelten gefunden, hier bauten die Römer ihr Kastell Abusinia, und von hier aus erstreckte sich der Limes, ein 600 Kilometer langer Wall gegen die Germanen, nach Westen in Richtung Rhein. Auch das älteste Kloster Bayerns, Kloster Weltenburg, das bereits um 600 von Wandermönchen aus den Vogesen gegründet wurde, steht hier. Und ganz in der Nähe thront auf dem Michelsberg die Befreiungshalle, die Bayerns König Ludwig I. erbauen ließ, zur Erinnerung an die Kriege gegen Napoleon – an denen Bayern teilgenommen hatte, nachdem es rechtzeitig vor Napoleons Niedergang auf die Seite seiner Gegner gewechselt war. Kolossal wirkt diese Befreiungshalle, wenn man unmittelbar davor steht, irgendwie überdimensioniert. Erst aus der Luft wird deutlich, wie sie sich in die Landschaft der umliegenden Hügel einfügt.

Der Flug über Bayern gibt noch viel mehr Blicke frei auf die jahrhundertealte Geschichte dieses Landes. Etwa auf Nürnberg, die Stadt von Hans Sachs und Albrecht Dürer: Aus der Vogelperspektive sieht man sofort, wie sich das mittelalterliche Nürnberg neben der Burg als freie Reichsstadt und dann über deren Stadtmauern hinaus entwickelte. Oder auf Landshut und Ingolstadt, deren bauliche

Lichtenfels

the air can you see how well it actually blends into the landscape of the surrounding hills.

A flight over Bavaria offers even more views into the centuries-old history of this land. For instance, there is Nuernberg, the city of Hans Sachs and Albrecht Duerer. From a bird's-eye view you can see how medieval Nuernberg developed as a free imperial city, first up around the hill and then as it expanded beyond the city walls. Or Landshut and Ingolstadt, whose architectural splendour still bears witness to their histories as seats of royal government, when the Wittelsbachs temporarily split into several dynastic lines in the 14th and 15th centuries. And who can forget the »Fairy Tale King« Ludwig II and the magnificent dreams he transformed into stone? These are some compelling reasons for the flourishing tourist-trade in Bavaria. Pre-eminent among these is Neuschwanstein, the most fantastical of all of Ludwig's castles, high on a cliff over Fuessen, and even more impressive when seen from up above than from down below. You will also see a more recent architectural monument: Munich's Olympic Stadium. When its unique tent roof is viewed from above, it gives the impression of airy lightness, as though a finely-woven spider's web hovered over the landscape like a giant canopy.

Finally, the vista from Launer's airplane offers a new view of »Bavaria Sancta« – the land of the Counter Reformation, with its churches and monastaries, chapels and roadside crosses. The only way that you can fully comprehend the enormous Ettal monastery complex is from a distance and it is not until you see the scenery of the entire Ammergauer Mountain range that you discover how Dominikus Zimmermann, the master builder of the Wieskirche, carefully echoed the contours of the mountains in the curves of his church. If you want to experience the glory of the heavens, step into the light-drenched interior of the Wieskirche and gaze up towards its pastel-coloured ceiling frescoes. If, however, you ascend to the skies with Gerhard Launer and cast your eyes back down towards the earth, you will have the privilege of experiencing all the worldly splendour of Bavaria. Perhaps then you will understand the Bavarian at the beginning of this introduction, the one who sat and looked out over the landscape, so utterly content. And you will know why it is that, if you ask him what makes him feel so content, he will tell you with inimitable understatement, that it is »halt scho scheh« here – simply so beautiful, so unique, and so unsurpassable.

Pracht noch heute davon zeugt, dass sie einst Residenzstädte waren, als sich die regierenden Wittelsbacher im 14./15. Jahrhundert vorübergehend in verschiedene Herrscherlinien aufspalteten. Nicht zu vergessen die Stein gewordenen Träume des Märchenkönigs Ludwig II., die mit ein Grund sind für den blühenden Tourismus in Bayern: vor allem Neuschwanstein, das fantastischste aller Ludwig-Schlösser, auf einem Felsen über Füssen thronend und, aus der Luft betrachtet, vielleicht noch imposanter als von unten. Und ein Baudenkmal aus jüngerer Zeit, das Münchener Olympiastadion mit seinem einzigartigen Zeltdach, vermittelt erst von oben den Eindruck einer luftigen Leichtigkeit, so als würde sich ein riesiges, fein gesponnenes Baldachinspinnennetz über die Landschaft legen.

Schließlich bietet der Blick aus dem Flugzeug auch eine andere Sicht auf Bavaria Sancta – das Land der Gegenreformation mit all seinen Kirchen und Klöstern, Kapellen und Wegkreuzen. So kann man nur aus der Distanz die mächtige Klosteranlage von Ettal als Ganzes erfassen. Und erst vor der Kulisse der Ammergauer Berge entdeckt man, wie der Baumeister Dominikus Zimmermann die Konturen der Wieskirche dem Auf und Ab der Hügel nachempfunden hat.

Wer einen Eindruck von der Herrlichkeit des Himmels bekommen möchte, der muss das lichtdurchflutete Innere der Wieskirche besuchen und zu den pastellfarbenen Deckenfresken hinaufsehen. Wer sich dagegen mit Gerhard Launer in den Himmel begibt und von dort einen Blick nach unten wirft, der darf die ganze irdische Herrlichkeit Bayerns erleben. Und er wird vielleicht verstehen, was den eingangs zitierten Bayern, der übers Land schaut, so zufrieden macht. Und warum er auf Nachfrage wohl mit unnachahmlichem Understatement antworten würde, dass es hier »halt scho scheh« ist – also ganz einmalig und unübertrefflich.

München, das etwas andere Dorf

Die Münchner sind wetterfühlig. Immer wenn Föhn ist, geht es ihnen besonders schlecht. Oder besonders gut. Oder auch so wie immer. Der warme Fallwind, der die Alpen herunterstreicht, ruft bei den einen Migräne und Depressionen hervor, bei den anderen euphorische Feel-good-Gefühle. Und die dritten merken gar nicht, dass Föhn ist. Höchstens daran, dass alle anderen ständig darüber reden – oder an der guten Aussicht.

Föhntage mit ihrer klaren Luft sind eine einmalige Gelegenheit, von einem erhöhten Ausguckposten aus, etwa dem Olympiaturm, die sechzig Kilometer südlich gelegene Alpenkette zu betrachten. Und nichts kann die Aussicht verstellen, seit München wieder einmal seinem Ruf als »Millionendorf« gerecht wurde und per Bürgerentscheid festlegte, dass kein Haus höher als die Türme der Frauenkirche sein dürfen.

Tatsächlich ist es Deutschlands drittgrößter Stadt gelungen, ihren besonderen »ländlichen« Charme zu bewahren, trotz eines rasanten wirtschaftlichen Aufschwungs und eifriger Bautätigkeit in den vergangenen Jahrzehnten. München ist noch immer überschaubarer als viele andere Millionenstädte, kleinteiliger, geordneter, gemütlicher, genießerischer, leiser, gelassener – und grüner. Nicht nur der riesige Englische Garten und die über achtzig Biergärten laden hier zum Durchatmen oder, wie man in Bayern sagen würde: zum Durchschnaufen ein.

All das ist wohl ein Grund dafür, dass diese selbst ernannte »Weltstadt mit Herz« und »nördlichste Stadt Italiens« bundesweit so begehrt ist. Umfragen zufolge würde jeder dritte Deutsche gerne in München leben.

Zugleich ist dieses heimelige »Dorf« aber auch eine Stadt der Superlative – zumindest fast: Es ist Deutschlands zweitgrößte Industriestadt und nach New York die zweitgrößte Verlagsstadt der Welt. Und es hat kulturelle Highlights von Weltformat, wie etwa den klassizistischen Prachtboulevard der Ludwigstraße, die Kunstsammlungen in den Pinakotheken oder die Philharmoniker. Es kann mit dem Deutschen Museum das größte Technikmuseum Europas vorweisen. Und jedes Jahr im September beginnt hier das Oktoberfest, das allergrößte Volksfest der Welt, wenn nicht der ganzen Milchstraße.

Munich, the village with a difference

The people of Munich are highly weather sensitive. Whenever the so-called »Foehn« arrives, they feel particularly bad. Or particularly good. Or the same as ever. This warm wind that blows down from the Alps causes migraines and depression in some people, and euphoric spirits in others. A third group of people does not even notice when the Foehn is there. At most they become aware of it when they hear everyone else talking about it – or when they see the fantastic view that always accompanies it.

Foehn days, with their uniquely clean air, give a unique opportunity to see the Alps sixty kilometers south of Munich. For an exceptionally good view, try climbing the Olympic Tower. Nothing can ruin the view from here, ever since Munich passed a law that no new building could be built higher than the spires of the Frauenkirche (Church of Our Lady).

In spite of a booming economy and fervent building activity in the last few decades, Germany's third largest city has truly succeeded in maintaining its rural charm. It is still far easier to get a good overview of Munich than of any other city of a million inhabitants or more. This is because Munich is divided into smaller, more manageable neighbourhoods, and is better ordered, more cosy, more pleasure-seeking, quieter, more relaxed, and greener than other cities. The enormous English Garden in downtown Munich, along with the city's 80-plus beer gardens, are not the only things that invite you to inhale deeply, or, as they say in Bavaria, »durchschnaufen«.

These are only a few of the reasons why this self-described »World City with a Heart« and »most northern Italian city« is so desirable throughout Germany. According to surveys, every third German would like to live in Munich. At the same time, this homey »village« is also a city of superlatives: it is Germany's second biggest industrial city, and, after New York, the second biggest publishing centre in the world. In addition to this, it has world class cultural highlights, such as the Ludwigstrasse (a magnificent classical boulevard); the extensive art collections of the Pinakothek galleries; and the Munich Philharmonic. The Deutsches Museum is the largest technical museum in all of Europe. And of course nobody can forget the Oktoberfest, the biggest beer festival in the world, which begins every September.

Gottes Haus im Häusermeer

Groß, gelb und hochbarock: Münchens Theatinerkirche aus dem 17. Jahrhundert und das angefügte Kloster sind das Werk der italienischen Baumeister Agostino Barelli und Enrico Zuccalli. Die Fassade kam erst hundert Jahre später dazu und repräsentiert spätes Rokoko.

God's House in a sea of houses

Grand, golden, and High Baroque: Munich's 17th century Theatinerkirche and the monastery attached to it are the work of Italian architects Agostino Barelli and Enrico Zuccalli. However, the façade was built 100 years later in the late Rococo style.

Im Bau
Das neue Stadion in Fröttmaning für die Fußball-Weltmeisterschaft 2006

Under Construction
The new stadion in Fröttmaning for the football world cup in 2006

Olympische Zelte
1972 wurde München olympisch. Geblieben ist der Stadt
eine Sportanlage von weithin gerühmter Eleganz. Auf 75 000
Quadratmetern Fläche überspannen Zeltdächer aus Acryl
das Olympiastadion, die Olympiahalle und das Schwimm-
stadion. 1700 Kilometer Stahlseile halten die luftigen Dächer
in der Schwebe.

Olympian tents
In 1972, Munich hosted the Olympic Games. Its legacy
to the city is a sports complex known far and wide for its
modern architectural elegance. Spanning a total area of
75,000 square meters, tent-like roofs made of acrylic canvas
cover the Olympic Stadium, the Olympic Hall, and the
Aquatic Centre. An astonishing 1,700 kilometers of steel
rods holds the airy roofs aloft.

Münchens Badewanne

So wird der sagenumwobene Starnberger
See bisweilen etwas despektierlich genannt.
Früher war er der »Fürstensee«: Erst baute
der Adel seine Schlösser an die Ufer, dann der
Geldadel seine Villen. Und dass – unter noch
immer ungeklärten Umständen – beim Seeort
Berg der Märchenkönig Ludwig ertrank, verleiht dem See für monarchistische Nostalgiker
fast die Aura von Weihwasser.

Munich's bathtub

This is what people sometimes call the Starnbergersee – albeit somewhat disrespectfully.
At one time it was known as »The Princes'
Lake«, after the noblemen who first built their
castles on its shores (and who were followed,
in turn, by the nouveau riche and their villas).
The fact that the »Fairy Tale King« Ludwig II
drowned near the lakeside town of Berg, under
circumstances that remain unexplained to
this day, lends the lake an aura of holiness for
nostalgic monarchists.

Ice age abrasions

Like the Chiemsee (left), the Ostersee lakes (top) are a remnant of the last ice age. Today's marshy nature-reserves actually emerged 12,000 years ago out of so-called »dead ice« – huge blocks of ice that splintered off and were left behind when the glaciers receded. These heavy masses pushed down into the earth, as far as the groundwater, which is still the primary source for nineteen pools, ponds, and lakes today.

Eiszeitliche Schürfwunden

Wie der Chiemsee (links), so sind auch die Osterseen (oben) ein Überbleibsel der Eiszeit. Das moorige Naturschutzgebiet entstand vor 12 000 Jahren aus Toteis – großen Eisblöcken, die abbrachen und liegen blieben, als sich die Gletscher auf den Rückzug machten. Die schweren Klumpen drückten sich in den Boden ein, bis hinab zum Grundwasser, aus dem noch heute die 19 Tümpel, Weiher und Seen gespeist werden.

Brücke zum Wohlstand

Der Inn zieht eine magische Schleife um Wasserburg. Und wie so oft in mittelalterlichen Städtechroniken nachzulesen, gründete sich auch Wasserburgs Wohlstand, von schmucken Bürgerhäusern noch heute bezeugt, auf Brückenzoll. Seit dem 12. Jahrhundert wurden hier die Salzspediteure aus Reichenhall kräftig abkassiert.

Bridge of prosperity

The Inn River draws a magical loop around Wasserburg. As one can often read in the medieval town chronicles, Wasserburg's prosperity was built on bridge tolls. Ever since the 12th century, salt shippers from Reichenhall were charged heavy tolls. Today, the town's historical good fortune is still evident in the pretty burgher houses from that period.

Der Stoff, aus dem die Ansichtskarten sind

Die Chiemgauer Alpen bei Frasdorf – schneeüberpudert an einem klirrend kalten Tag. Diese Übergangslandschaft zwischen hügeligem, gletschergeformtem Flachland und Hochgebirge bestätigt eine alte Weisheit der Landschaftsästhetik: Oft sind die Grenzen und Übergänge das Spannendste und Spektakulärste.

Postcard dreams

The Chiemgauer Alps at Frasdorf, covered with a dusting of snow on an icy-cold day. This landscape, which contains both hilly, glacier-carved countryside and high mountains, confirms an old landscaping wisdom that transitional areas are often the most exciting and spectacular.

The »Bavarian Sea«

This is what locals lovingly call the Chiemsee, although its water is no saltier than that of any other lake. They call it a sea for its sheer size; at 80 square kilometers the Chiemsee is Bavaria's biggest lake. The only German lakes that exceed it in size are the Mueritzsee (109 square kilometers) in Mecklenburg-Vorpomerania and Lake Constance (571 square kilometers), which, as an international body of water, cannot really be counted.

The Chiemsee is more than 70 meters deep. Its floor was carved out during the last ice age by gigantic glacial masses. Its northern, western, and eastern shores form a huge, almost horseshoe-shaped, moraine. Its southern shore is flat and marshy, where the Tyrolian River Ache, the most substantial affluent of the Chiemsee, pushes its delta forward. Together with the Chiemsee's second affluent, the River Priem, the Ache has already filled two-thirds of the Chiemsee with sand and other debris since the last ice age ended. Each year this creates another two hectares of land, so that it is only a matter of time before the Chiemsee looks just as it did before the last ice age.

Until then, there should be no more doubt, even north of Bavaria, how the name »Chiemsee« is pronounced. It doesn't begin with a »ch« or even a »sch«, but with a »k« sound, as in »chemistry« or »Christmas«. This issue of pronunciation is not open to debate with Bavarians!

Das Bayerische Meer

So wird der Chiemsee liebevoll von den Einheimischen genannt, obwohl sein Wasser kein bisschen mehr Salz enthält als andere Seen. Der Name kommt von der schieren Größe, denn immerhin ist der Chiemsee mit 80 Quadratkilometern Bayerns größter See und wird in Deutschland nur übertroffen vom Müritzsee (109 qm) in Mecklenburg-Vorpommern und vom Bodensee (571 qm), der als internationales Gewässer außer Konkurrenz läuft.

Über 70 Meter tief ist der Chiemsee. Sein Grund wurde während der letzten Eiszeit von gewaltigen Gletschermassen ausgehobelt. Das Ufer nach Norden, Westen und Osten bildet ein riesiger Moränenring. Das Südufer ist flach und moorig; hier schiebt die Tiroler Ache, der wasserreichste Zufluss des Chiemsees, ihr Delta vor. Gemeinsam mit dem zweiten Zufluss, der Priem, hat sie seit der Eiszeit bereits zwei Drittel des Chiemsees mit Sand und Geröll aufgeschüttet. Jährlich verlanden weitere 200 Hektar, so dass es nur noch eine Frage der Zeit ist, bis es am Chiemsee wieder so aussieht wie vor der Eiszeit.

Bis dahin besteht dann vielleicht auch nördlich von Bayern kein Zweifel mehr darüber, wie der Name »Chiemsee« ausgesprochen wird. Er beginnt nicht etwa mit »Ch« oder gar »Sch«, sondern mit »K« – genau wie »Chemie« oder »China«, worüber der Bayer ja auch nicht mit sich diskutieren lässt.

Insel im Strom der Zeit

Um 722 soll Herzog Tassilo eine Benediktiner-
abtei auf der Fraueninsel im Chiemsee ge-
stiftet haben. Seither ist das Eiland fest in der
Hand der Gottesdiener und -dienerinnen.
Heute sind es allerdings zum wenigsten
fromme Pilger, die per Dampfer an die Wir-
kungsstätte der Heiligen Irmgard (866 gestor-
ben) kommen; Touristen wollen die Landschaft oder das Essen genießen oder einfach
einen der letzten Orte der Welt, an dem
keine Autos fahren dürfen.

An island in the river of time

It is said that Duke Tassilo founded a Benedictine abbey on the Fraueninsel in the Chiemsee around 722 A. D. Since then, the island
has been safe in the hands of the servants of
God. Today, however, very few of its visitors
are devout pilgrims, as they travel by steam-
ship to where St. Irmgard (d. 866 A. D.) did her
holy work. Instead, most tourists wish either
to enjoy the landscape and food, or simply to
experience one of the last places in the world
where cars are banned.

Hoch im Kurs bei Kurgästen

Lang wie die ehemalige Gletscherzunge, die ihn schuf, erstreckt sich der Tegernsee zwischen den Alpen nach Norden. Er ist mit 72 Metern zwar genauso tief, aber von der Fläche her nur ein Neuntel so groß wie der Chiemsee. Trotzdem steht er ebenso hoch im Kurs bei Tagesausflüglern, Urlaubern oder Kurenden – und der Heil- und Kurort Bad Wiessee natürlich vor allem bei Zockern.

High marks with spa visitors

The Tegernsee extends northward between the Alps, as long as the glacial masses that carved it out so many years ago. At 72 meters, it is just as deep as the Chiemsee, but only one ninth as big in area. Nevertheless, the Tegernsee is equally highly rated by day-trippers, holiday-makers, and spa visitors – especially the health- and spa-resort Bad Wiessee, which is particularly beloved by gamblers.

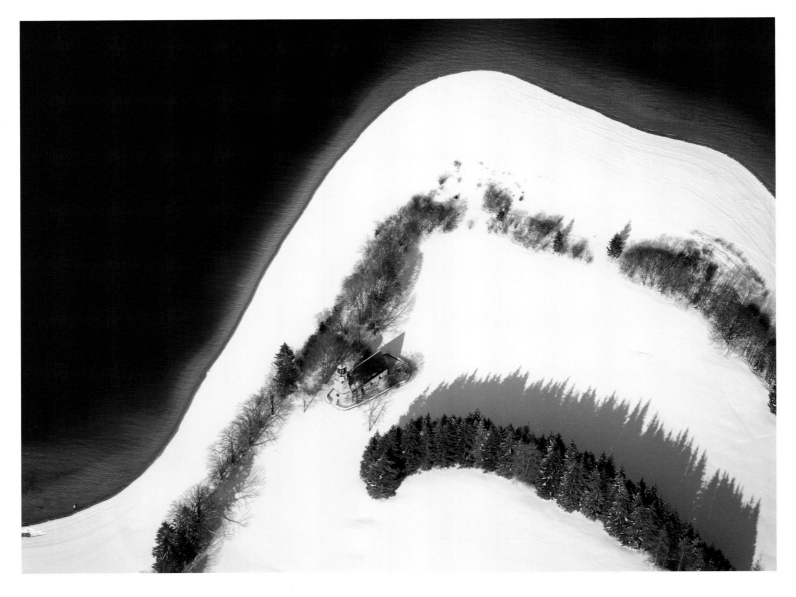

How firm a foundation

Testaments to Bavarian piety can still be found on remote country lanes or in other isolated locations in the form of a »Marterl« (a roadside crucifix) or a chapel, such as this one here on the shore of the Walchensee.

Das Seeufer als Fundament des Glaubens

Zeugen bayerischer Frömmigkeit finden sich noch an den einsamsten Feldwegen und abgeschiedensten Orten – in Form eines »Marterls« (Wegkreuz) oder einer Kapelle, wie hier am Ufer des Walchensees.

A castle for science

Schloss Ringberg is the most distinguished address of Germany's Max Planck Society. The castle was built by Duke Luitpold of Bavaria (1890–1973), with deliberate reference to Neuschwanstein. The nobleman, who had studied philosophy and art history, had his stone castle built according to the historical design of its great forbear, erected by King Ludwig II, high upon a cliff. While the magnificent Schloss Ringberg did not cost a cent of public money, it cost Luitpold his entire personal fortune.

Ein Schloss für die Wissenschaft

Heute ist Schloss Ringberg die vornehmste Adresse der deutschen Max-Planck-Gesellschaft. Erbaut wurde die Anlage, die nach dem Vorbild Neuschwansteins geplant war, vom Bayernherzog Luitpold (1890–1973). Der adelige studierte Philosoph und Kunstgeschichtler ließ sein Schloss nach dem historischen Muster der Hochburgen in Stein setzen. Der Prachtbau verschlang zwar kein Staats-, dafür aber Luitpolds gesamtes Privatvermögen.

Alpensee von Menschenhand

Ohne ihn müssten die Münchner Hochwasser-
wetter fürchten: Der Sylvensteinsee, südlich
von Lenggries in den Nördlichen Kalkalpen
gelegen, ist ein vier Quadratkilometer großes
Staubecken der Isar. Seine Hauptaufgabe ist es,
den Wasserstand des Flusses zu regulieren:
bei Flutwetter die Wassermassen aus den
Bergen aufzufangen und in heißen Sommern
die Isar vor dem Austrocknen zu bewahren.

A man-made alpine lake

Without it, the people of Munich would be
in danger of floods. The Sylvensteinsee, south
of Lenggries in the northern Limestone Alps,
is a four kilometer square reservoir of the
Isar. Its main function is to regulate the water
level of the river by collecting the mountain
run-off during the spring melt, and protect-
ing the Isar from drying out during the hot
summers.

A fine kettle of fish

In the Aischgrund (top) and Aurachtal valleys (photo right), you can see kilometer upon kilometer of fish ponds. Every fifth carp that grows to maturity in Germany is cultivated in one of these man-made bodies of water, for which the Middle Franconian landscape is well known. The harvest happens in late autumn: the fish are moved into large vats, where they spend their last few weeks before landing on the table for a traditional Christmas or New Year's dinner.

Felder für die Fischernte

Im Aischgrund (oben) und im Aurachtal (Bild rechts) reiht sich kilometerweit Fischteich an Fischteich. Jeder fünfte in Deutschland herangewachsene Karpfen schwamm in einem der Kunstgewässer, für die diese mittelfränkische Landschaft bekannt ist. ›Erntezeit‹ ist im späten Herbst. Dann heißt es umziehen in Bottiche, wo diese traditionellen Weihnachts- und Silvesterfische ihre letzten Wochen vor dem festlichen Ende verbringen.

The »Wies« – almost as famous as the »Wies'n«

If you want to experience Bavarian beer bliss, you have to go to the »Wies'n« (Oktoberfest). But if you want to experience the apogee of Rococo architecture, you cannot afford to miss the Wieskirche (right), lovingly known as »the Wies« for short. Then, if you need an antidote to all its stucco and gold-plated ornament, we suggest you turn to the architecture of nature, and head for the gothic peaks of the High Alps, for example, those surrounding the Kochelsee (top) and the Walchensee (top, in the background).

Die Wies – fast so berühmt wie die Wies'n

Wer bayerische Bierseligkeit will, muss auf die »Wies'n« (Oktoberfest), wer Rokoko-Baukunst in Vollendung sehen will, besucht die Wieskirche (rechts), kurz und liebevoll »die Wies« genannt. Und wer nach all dem Stuck und blattgoldenen Zierrat den Kontrast im Bereich der Naturbauwerke sucht, der nähere sich – zum Beispiel über Kochelsee (oben) und Walchensee (oben im Hintergrund) – den gotischen Spitzen des alpinen Hochgebirges.

Der Weg ist das Ziel

Viele kommen nur zum Eibsee, um von hier aus hinauf zum höchsten deutschen Gipfel zu entschweben. Doch der knapp tausend Meter hoch gelegene kristallene See hat mehr zu bieten als eine Gondelstation: einen idyllischen Rundwanderweg mit atemberaubendem Fernblick auf die Zugspitze und ihre felsigen Nachbarn.

Onwards and upwards ...

Many people only come to the Eibsee so they can ascend from here to the highest peak in Germany (the Zugspitze). But the crystalline lake, which is just short of 1,000 meters above sea level, has more to offer than a cable-car base station. It also has an idyllic hiking trail that goes right around the lake, complete with a breathtaking view of the Zugspitze and its craggy neighbours.

53

Politik braucht Symbole

Nach dieser Maxime handelte schon Ludwig der Bayer: 1330, gerade eben aus Rom von seiner Krönung zum ersten Wittelsbacher Kaiser heimgekehrt, gründete er das Kloster Ettal. Der Name war damals in der Hochzeit päpstlicher Weltherrschaftsansprüche ein Politikum: Ettal = Ehe-Tal. Symbolisch in Stein gesetzt werden sollte das Bündnis von Kaiser und Mutter Maria, von weltlicher Macht und Himmelsmacht. Erst vierhundert Jahre später bekam die einst gotische Klosterkirche ihr heutiges Gesicht eines barocken Kuppelbaus.

Politics needs symbols

Ludwig the Bavarian already acted in accordance with this motto long ago: in 1330 A.D., after returning from Rome where he had been crowned as the first Emperor from the House of Wittelsbach, he founded the Ettal monastery. At a time when papal claims to world domination were at their peak, the name he gave to this monastery was a political act: Ettal = Ehe-Tal, or »wedding valley«. The alliance between Holy Roman Emperor and Mary, Mother of God, between earthly and heavenly power, was symbolically set into stone here. This formerly Gothic monastery church did not receive its Baroque cupola until 400 years later, which we can still see today.

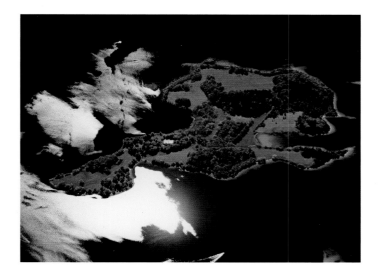

Everything flows...

If Heraclitus had been a Bavarian Swabian and had picked the Lech River as the model for his natural philosophy, his famous saying, »everything flows«, might have been »everything is dammed«. Since the beginning of the 19th century, the river has been harnessed as a source of power, its natural flow slowed down by a series of dams. Numerous nature reserves surrounding the Forggensee reservoir (left side) or the Upper Lechsee (top left) are proof that human intervention in nature does not necessarily lead to the destruction of the natural world.

Alles fließt bis zur nächsten Staustufe

Wäre Heraklit ein bayerischer Schwabe gewesen und hätte sich den Lech als Vorbild für seine Naturphilosophie ausgewählt, so wäre aus dem berühmten »Alles fließt« vielleicht ein »Alles staut sich« geworden. Bereits seit Ende des 19. Jahrhunderts wird dieser Fluss zur Stromgewinnung genutzt und durch zahlreiche Staustufen immer wieder abgebremst. Dass der Eingriff durch die Menschen nicht zwangsläufig zur Verschandelung der Landschaft führen muss, beweisen die vielen Naturgebiete, etwa rund um das Staubecken des Forggensees (linke Seite) oder des Oberen Lechsees (oben links).

Both copy and original

A few years ago, the magazine GEO commissioned seven prominent photographers to take pictures of Neuschwanstein, »the most photographed-to-death object in all of Germany«. Some refused, saying that the castle had already become a visual cliché: it was a three-dimensional postcard and there was no need to transform it into a two-dimensional one. Others accepted this Bavarian tourism hotspot just as they found it, the castle posed like a model in front of the scenic backdrop of mountain and forest. No matter how you feel about Neuschwanstein, this most spectacular of King Ludwig's three castles does not need to be staged-directed. Instead, its cumulative impact increases from each new point-of-view, even from this bird's-eye view.

When Ludwig started to build the castle in 1868, his contemporaries thought it looked like a romanticized copy of medieval models, borrowing arbitrarily as it does from Romanesque, Gothic, and Byzantine art and architecture. But meanwhile, Neuschwanstein has long since developed into an unmistakable original in the eyes of the world, and is even imitated by others, as can now be seen in the Florida and Paris Disneylands.

Kopie und Original zugleich

Vor einigen Jahren beauftragte die Zeitschrift GEO sieben prominente Fotografen damit, Neuschwanstein, »das totfotografierteste Objekt in Deutschland«, jeweils in ihrer Auffassung abzulichten. Die einen verweigerten sich dem Klischee mit der Begründung, das Schloss sei eine dreidimensionale Postkarte, also solle man nicht versuchen, eine zweidimensionale Postkarte daraus zu machen. Andere akzeptierten den bayerischen Tourismus-Hotspot so, wie er ist, und ließen das Schloss einfach nur vor der Wald- und Bergkulisse Modell stehen.

Was auch immer man über Neuschwanstein denken mag, dieses spektakulärste der drei Ludwig-Schlösser muss nicht inszeniert werden, sondern entfaltet aus jedem Blickwinkel seine Wirkung, selbst aus der Vogelperspektive.

Als das Schloss ab 1868 gebaut wurde, erschien es Ludwigs Zeitgenossen als eine romantisierende Kopie mittelalterlicher Vorbilder, die sich willkürlich bei der Romanik, der Gotik und der byzantinischen (Bau-)Kunst bediente. Inzwischen hat sich Neuschwanstein in der Sicht der Welt längst zum unverwechselbaren Original gemausert – und wurde seinerseits immer wieder kopiert, wie in den Disneylands von Florida und Paris.

Wie der Sohn, so der Vater

Kein Ludwig-Schloss, sondern ein Bau seines
Vaters und Vorgängers Maximilian II., der
Hohenschwangau bei Füssen auf den Funda-
menten eines älteren Vorgängerbaus errich-
ten ließ. Hier verfasste Ludwig II. im Jahr 1870
seinen Kaiserbrief, in dem er die deutschen
Fürsten aufforderte, Preußens Wilhelm die
Kaiserwürde anzutragen – und wurde dafür
von Preußen so fürstlich belohnt, dass er
das Vaterschloss Hohenschwangau mit Neuschwanstein noch toppen konnte.

Like father, like son

This is not one of King Ludwig's castles,
rather it was erected by his father and prede-
cessor Maximilian II, who built the castle of
Hohenschwangau near Fuessen on the foun-
dations of an earlier building. It is, however,
where Ludwig II composed his famous »Emperor's Letter« in 1870, in which he urged the
German princes to confer the title of Emperor
onto Wilhelm of Prussia, an act for which Ludwig was so generously rewarded by Prussia
that he was then able to surpass his father's
Hohenschwangau with his own castle, Neuschwanstein.

Schön grün, schön sahnig

»Ich habe Bayern groß gemacht«, sagte Napoleon, nachdem er Anfang des 19. Jahrhunderts den Kurfürsten Maximilian IV. Joseph zum König Maximilian I. und das Land Bayern zum Königreich erhoben hatte, »ich kann es noch größer machen.« Sprach's und verdoppelte Bayerns Staatsgebiet, indem er ihm Franken und Schwaben zuschlug. Seitdem ist der größere, östliche Teil des Allgäus bayerisch, der westliche württembergisch, und das Kleine Walsertal ist österreichisches Staatsgebiet.

Der Name »Allgäu« ist sprachgeschichtlich umstritten; die meisten lesen darin eine mundartliche Umformung von »Alpgau«; dieser Name findet sich so schon in einer Urkunde aus dem Jahre 817. Die Allgäuer Alpen bilden einen Teil der nördlichen Kalkalpen und ragen bis zu 2657 Meter (Hoher Grottenkopf) auf. Die häufig gleichmäßig steil geneigten Grashänge begünstigen die Almwirtschaft, also die Form der Wirtschaft, die für das gesamte Allgäu kultur- und imagebildend war.

Ach, das Allgäu! Es gibt nur wenige deutsche Landschaftsnamen, die so eindeutig positive Bilder im Kopf freisetzen. Das ist doch dieses Land, wo Milch aus braunen, lang bewimperten Kühen fließt, zu üppigem Käse gerinnt und wo sich hinter sanft geschwungenen Wiesenhügeln die Nordalpenkette von ihrer besten Seite zeigt. Wo jeder Atemzug die Lungenbläschen jubeln lässt und die Sonne unermüdlich Überstunden macht.

Natürlich gibt es auch hier Skandale um Gülle im Grundwasser oder Massentierhaltung, und natürlich wird der Allgäuer Käse heute in der Regel nicht mehr oben auf der Alp zubereitet, wie die Alm im alemannischen Sprachraum heißt. Dennoch wird das Allgäu in unseren Köpfen immer ein Paradiesland bleiben. Und das völlig zu Recht, denn im Allgäu wird vielerorts ein sanfterer Tourismus gepflegt als etwa im überlaufenen Oberbayern. Hier werden alte Höfe behutsamer modernisiert, wird oft erhalten und restauriert statt abgerissen. Und auch die unrentabel gewordene Almwirtschaft wird subventioniert, um sie am Leben zu erhalten – denn schließlich machen erst die Alpen (Almen) die Alpen so richtig schön!

Nice and green, nice and creamy

»I made Bavaria great,« said Napoleon, »and I can make it even greater.« This was directly after he had elevated Elector Maximilian IV Joseph to the position of King Maximilian I at the beginning of the 19th century, in the process making Bavaria a Kingdom. With these words he doubled Bavaria's territory by adding Franconia and Swabia to it. Ever since then, the larger, eastern part of the Allgaeu has become Bavarian, the western part too, while the valley of Kleine Walsertal became part of Austria.

The etymology of the name »Allgaeu« is disputed. Most people believe that it is a vernacular transformation of »Alpgau«, a name that was documented as early as the year 817 A. D. The Allgaeuer Alps form part of the northern Limestone Alps and tower as high as 2,657 meters (the Hoher Grottenkopf peak). Their grassy slopes are often fairly even, making them favourable to the Alpine pastoral agriculture that has significantly shaped the culture and popular impression of the entire region.

Oh, the Allgaeu! Few German landscapes evoke such singularly positive images. After all, this is the land where milk flows from chocolate-brown cows with beautiful long eyelashes, where it is then transformed into rich cheese, and where the Northern Alps show their most attractive face behind softly rolling green hills. This is a place where every breath of air makes your lungs sing with joy, and where the sun shines tirelessly.

Naturally, the same scandals that exist elsewhere concerning animal run-off in the groundwater or factory farms also exist here and, of course, Allgaeu cheese is now only rarely made on the »Alp« (the name given to the »Alm«, or Alpine meadow in the area where the Alemannic dialect is spoken). Nevertheless, the Allgaeu continues to remain a paradise in people's imaginations. And rightly so, because a less intrusive form of tourism is practiced here than in Upper Bavaria, which has become entirely overrun. Here in the Allgaeu, old farms are often modernized with extreme care: maintained and restored instead of torn down. In addition, the now unprofitable Alpine pasture agriculture is subsidized to keep it alive, because, after all, it is the Allgaeuer Alps that make the entire mountain range so beautiful.

Füssen von Augsburgs Gnaden

Augsburgs Geistlichkeit setzte sich ab 1313 für fünf Jahrhunderte flussaufwärts in Füssen am Lech fest. Alles überragender Ausdruck ihres fürstbischöflichen Einflusses war das Benediktinerkloster St. Mang (Bildmitte rechts). Der Heilige Magnus – St. Mang ist gewissermaßen sein lokaler Kosename – missionierte im 8. Jahrhundert das Allgäu.

Fuessen – blessed by Augsburg's grace

For 500 years after 1313, Augsburg's clergy had its seat in Fuessen on the Lech River. The Benedictine monastery of St. Mang (in the middle of the photograph on the right) was the most outstanding physical expression of the influence of its prince-bishops. St. Magnus – St. Mang is his local nickname – was a missionary in the Allgaeu in the 8th century.

Ora et labora

Wie so viele Klöster in Bayern wurde auch die südöstlich von Memmingen gelegene Abtei von Ottobeuren im 8. Jahrhundert von Benediktinern gegründet. Ihre Maxime »Ora et labora!« (»Bete und arbeite!«) stammt in dieser griffigen Form zwar aus dem Spätmittelalter, geht sinngemäß aber zurück auf Benedikt von Nursia (ca. 480–547), den »Vater des Mönchstums«. Unter Experten gilt die Ottobeurer Abtei als eine der bedeutendsten barocken Klosteranlagen in ganz Europa.

Ora et labora – pray and work

Like many Bavarian cloisters, Ottobeuren Abbey, just south-east of Memmingen, was also founded by Benedictines. Although their pithy maxim »Ora et labora!« (»pray and work!«) has its origin in the late Middle Ages, its philosophy goes back as far as Benedict of Nursia (ca. 480–547 A. D.), known as the »Father of Monasticism«. Experts consider Ottobeuren Abbey to be one of the most important Baroque monastic structures in all of Europe.

Wo die Butterbörse steht

Bereits die Kelten hatten an einer Flusskrüm-
mung der Iller das Oppidum »Cambodunum«
gegründet. Zu Zeiten des Kaisers Tiberius
errichteten dann die Römer ganz in der Nähe
der Keltensiedlung eine Garnisonsstadt, die
bald zu einem wichtigen Handelszentrum der
Provinz Raetien heranwuchs. In neuerer Zeit
bestimmten Milchprodukte (Allgäuer Emmen-
taler) das Image der Stadt Kempten, in der
die Süddeutsche Butter- und Allgäuer Käse-
börse ihren Sitz hat.

Butter them up!

In early days the Celts had set up the fortified base of »Cambodunum« at a bend in the
Iller River. Then, around the time of Emperor
Tiberius, the Romans erected a garrison town
near this former Celtic settlement, and it soon
became one of the most important trade cen-
ters of the province Rhaetia. In more recent
times, milk products (especially Allgaeuer
Emmental) have shaped the image of the town
of Kempten, which is the headquarter of the
south German butter and cheese market.

As the name already suggests ...

Oberstdorf (»the highest village«) – which sits at the foot of
the Nebelhorn (2,224 meters) and the Fellhorn (2,037 meters) –
ranks right at the top of Bavarian hiking and winter sport
tourism hotspots, with an astonishing record of 2.5 million
overnight visitors per year.

Wie der Name schon sagt ...

... rangiert Oberstdorf, zu Füßen von Nebelhorn (2224
Meter) und Fellhorn (2037 Meter), ganz zuoberst im bayeri-
schen Wander- und Wintersporttourismus: 2,5 Millionen
Gästeübernachtungen pro Jahr, das ist Rekord.

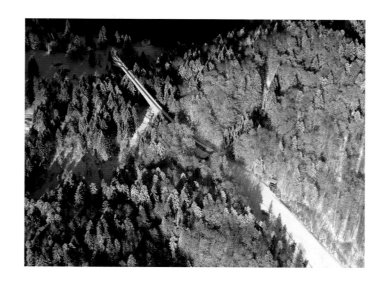

Bigger, higher, farther …

The huge ski-jump of Oberstdorf is unquestionably the best-known structure in the entire region. At the end of each year, the best ski-jumpers from around the world gather here. More than a million people across the globe have watched on television how, for example, Norway's Roar Ljockelsoey set the ski-jump record with his jump of 223 meters in 2004. Perhaps the world-wide fascination with this sport can be explained by the fact that, more than any other sport, it creates the illusion that human beings can rise above the laws of nature.

Oberstdorf is where the famous »Vierschanzentournee« (a tournament that involves four different ski-jumps) traditionally begins, followed by Garmisch-Partenkirchen, Innsbruck, and Bischofshofen. The tournament is a test of strength that we might call the »World Cup« of ski-jumping.

The original ski-jump of 1949 was replaced by a new construction made of reinforced concrete in 1973. However, it did not happen without heated discussion, because many people were emotionally attached to the striking original wooden structure. Ultimately safety (who could disagree with that?) triumphed over nostalgia, although the new structure retains the name of the local ski-jumper and architect of the 1949 version: Heini Klopfer.

Größer, höher, weiter

Die Skiflug-Großschanze von Oberstdorf ist mit Sicherheit das bekannteste Bauwerk der Region. Zu jedem Jahresende versammelt sich hier die Weltelite der Skispringer. Und ein Millionen-Fernsehpublikum rund um den Erdball schaut Fabelsprüngen zu, wie etwa dem des Norwegers Roar Ljokkelsoey, der hier mit seinem 223-Meter-Flug 2004 den Schanzenrekord aufstellte. Vielleicht liegt die globale Faszination dieser Sportart ja ganz einfach darin, dass sie mehr als andere Disziplinen die Illusion erzeugt, der Mensch könnte sich über die Naturgesetze erheben.

Oberstdorf bildet traditionell den Auftakt der Vierschanzentournee, gefolgt von Garmisch-Partenkirchen, Innsbruck und Bischofshofen, ein Kräftemessen, das so etwas wie die Weltmeisterschaft der Überflieger ist.

1973 wurde die ursprüngliche Schanze von 1949 durch eine Spannleichtbetonanlage ersetzt. Das ging nicht ganz ohne emotionsgeladene Diskussionen ab, denn bei vielen hing das Herz an der markanten Holzgestalt. Aber Sicherheit – wer wollte da widersprechen? – ging zuletzt vor Nostalgie. Immerhin, die Neugestalt behielt den Namen des einheimischen Skispringers und Architekten der 1949er-Schanze: Heini Klopfer.

A region for all seasons

The Allgaeu is one of the few German tourist regions that is »in season« all year round. Its rolling hills at the foot of the Alps are the number-one choice both for hikers and cross-country skiers. In addition, the churches there keep an open-door policy throughout the year for the benefit of religious art enthusiasts.

... und das nicht nur zur Sommerzeit

Das Allgäu ist eine der wenigen deutschen Urlaubsregionen, die fast das ganze Jahr über Saison haben. Unter Wanderern ebenso wie unter Skilangläufern gilt das Hügelland am Fuße der Alpen als erste Adresse. Und für die Liebhaber sakraler Kunst haben die Kirchen sowieso das ganze Jahr über Tag der offenen Tür.

Gott ist mit den Einsamen

Kloster Lanquaid an der Großen Laber liegt einsam auf weiter Flur, wie viele Kirchen und Kapellen im Bayernland. Wer sich Gott befahl und ein Leben hinter Klostermauern wählte, wollte zur Welt mit all ihren Verlockungen einen möglichst großen Abstand halten.

God is with the lonely

Like many churches and chapels in Bavaria, Kloster Lanquaid on the Grosser Laber River is isolated in the middle of a large field. Those who dedicated themselves to God and chose a life behind cloister walls were thus able to keep as distant as possible from worldly temptations.

73

The crystal waters of the Rhine

The water of Lake Constance is carefully monitored to maintain drinking-quality water, as Stuttgart draws upon the water of the Rhine that gathers in Lake Constance with a long steel straw or pipeline.

Rheinwasser – Reinwasser

Der Bodensee muss – sorgfältig überwacht – Trinkwasser-qualität behalten; denn Stuttgart trinkt mit überlangem stählernem Strohhalm das Rheinwasser, das sich im Boden-see sammelt.

Gentle winds over Lindau

Lindau's main landmark, a six-meter-high Bavarian lion at
the entrance to the harbour, proclaims the fact that the
town is Bavarian, situated as it is on the tiny tip of Bavarian
territory that extends between Austria and Baden-Wuerttemberg through the waters of Lake Constance to its shores.
At the same time, Lindau is also Bavaria's only island town.
Even today, the island, on which the old town with its pretty
burgher houses from the 16th and 17th centuries is located,
can only be reached by bridge.

Lindes Lüftchen über Lindau

Schon das Wahrzeichen der Stadt, ein sechs Meter hoher
bayerischer Löwe an der Hafeneinfahrt, verkündet, dass
Lindau auf dem kleinen Zipfelchen Land liegt, mit dem sich
Bayern zwischen Österreich und Baden-Württemberg hin-
durch bis ans Ufer des Bodensees erstreckt. Lindau ist
zugleich auch Bayerns einzige Inselstadt. Denn noch heute
ist die Insel, auf der die Altstadt mit ihren schmucken Bürgerhäusern aus dem 16. und 17. Jahrhundert liegt, nur über
eine Brücke zu erreichen.

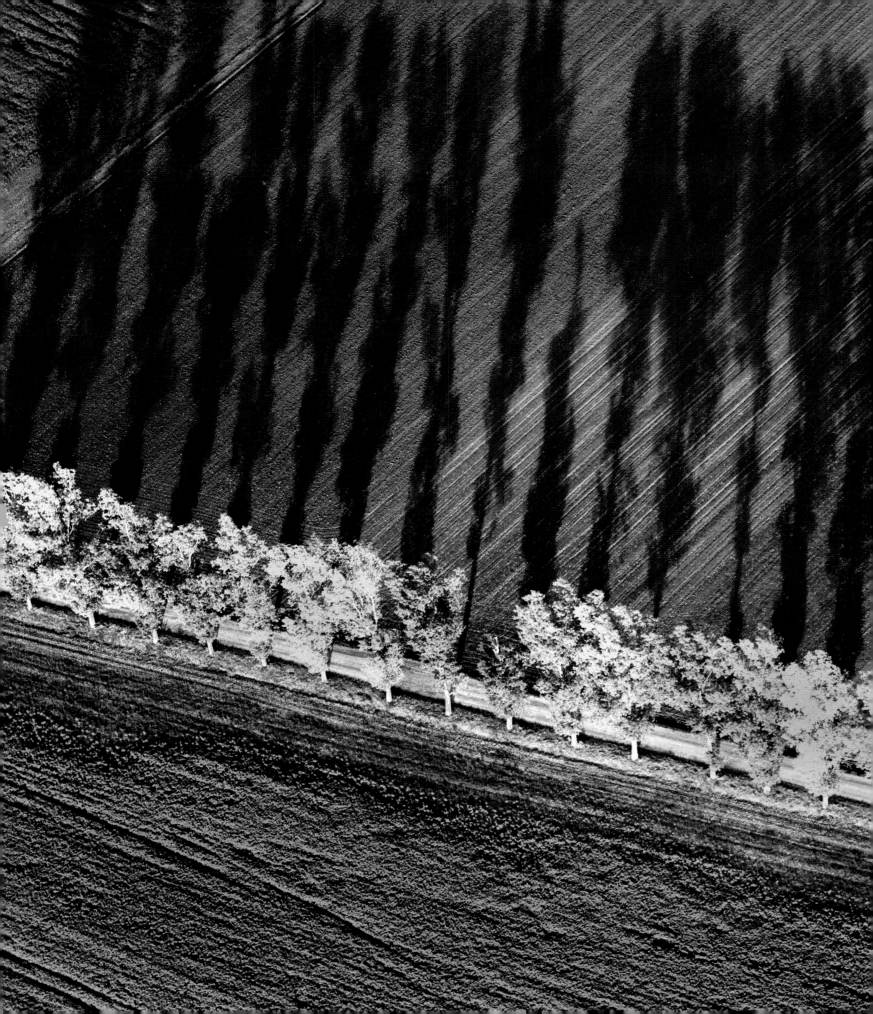

Does money corrupt?

Not necessarily! The fantastically rich citizen of Augsburg, Jakob Fugger, endowed his fellow citizens with the Fuggerei (right), a housing settlement for the poor that was named after him and, in so doing, laid the cornerstone of the social housing movement. Even today, the Fuggerei offers a place to live to those in need.

Be prepared to be bowled over by the building blocks at Legoland near Guenzburg (top). On days with high numbers of visitors, this plastic wonderland is fenced in by rows and rows of cars.

Verdirbt Geld den Charakter?

Nicht notwendigerweise! Der superreiche Augsburger Jakob Fugger stiftete 1516 den Augsburgern die Fuggerei (rechte Seite), eine nach ihm benannte Wohnsiedlung für Arme, und legte damit den Grundstein für den sozialen Wohnungsbau. Noch heute bietet die Fuggerei Bedürftigen eine Unterkunft.

»Bauklötze staunen« ist im Legoland bei Günzburg (oben) angesagt. An Tagen mit starkem Besucherandrang wird das Plastik-Wunderland von vielen Reihen Blech gesäumt.

Schläge ins Wasser …

… können erfolgreich sein, wie das Beispiel Ingolstadt beweist: Im 14. Jahrhundert sperrten die Ingolstädter den Donaustrom und zwangen den Schiffsverkehr in den Nordarm, auf den sie direkten – vor allem zollfiskalischen – Zugriff hatten. Schon zuvor hatte man eine vergleichbare »Standortverbesserung« gewagt: Die Schutter wurde zum Siedlungsbereich umgeleitet, um Mühlen zu drehen.

Mit dieser frühen Zwangsverpflichtung von Fluss und Nebenfluss hatte Ingolstadt seinen Aufstieg zur Metropole am Donauoberlauf begründet, sich aber auch periodisch wiederkehrendes Ungemach in die Stadt geholt. Die Schutter war nicht nur eine Arbeitsmagd, die Schleifsteine drehte und Pferde wusch (Ross-Schwemme), sie nahm sich immer mal wieder die Freiheit zu unkontrollierten Stadtausflügen.

Zu Recht ist Ingolstadt stolz auf seinen liebevoll restaurierten mittelalterlichen Stadtkern. Reste der Stadtmauer erzählen noch davon, dass es im 16. Jahrhundert eine der bestbefestigten Städte Bayerns war. Heute ist Ingolstadt als wichtiger Automobilstandort ein Bollwerk der deutschen Industrie.

Working with water …

Interfering with the flow of nature can actually be very successful, as the example of Ingolstadt proves. In the 14th century, Ingolstadt's citizens blocked the Danube and redirected all its ship traffic into the Nordarm River, which they controlled, most significantly, for the purpose of collecting tariffs and tolls. Even before that, the people of Ingolstadt had made a similar »improvement« to their town – they redirected the Schutter River to settled areas in order to power local mills.

This forced conscription of rivers initiated Ingolstadt's rise to a metropolis on the Upper Danube, but also occasioned some disasters. The Schutter turned out to be more than a docile maid, happy rotating grindstones and washing horses (Ross-Schwemme) all day. Occasionally she decided to go on a rampage through the middle of town.

Ingolstadt has every right to be proud of its lovingly restored medieval old town centre. Remnants of the old wall still remind visitors that it was once one of the best fortified towns in Bavaria. Today, as an important site of car manufacturing, Ingolstadt is one of the bulwarks of German industry.

Ingolstadt near and far

Ingolstadt nah und fern

»Bier auf Wein, das lass sein«?

One could translate this folk saying as: »If you drink beer after wine, you won't feel so fine.« It warns of the consequences of drinking alcoholic beverages in the wrong order at mealtimes. But it does not necessarily hold true in the world of agriculture: the Hallertau (Haller Valley), was full of vineyards before it became an area for growing hops. Now it is the largest area for hops cultivation anywhere, with 20 per cent of the world's hops grown in this single area north of Munich. Farther north, the Altmuehl River continues to meander in wide curves through the Altmuehltal (Altmuehl Valley), Germany's biggest nature park.

Bier auf Wein, das lass sein?

So reimt der Volksmund und warnt damit vor den gesundheitlichen Folgen einer falschen Getränkefolge bei Tisch. Für die agrarische Nutzung muss das aber wohl nicht gelten: Die Hallertau, vulgo Holledau, war Weinland, bevor sie Hopfenland wurde – und dann gleich das größte zusammenhängende Anbaugebiet überhaupt: 20 Prozent der Welt-Hopfenernte sichert allein dieser Landstrich nördlich von München.

Im Norden angrenzend darf die Altmühl (links) noch wie eh und je in engen und weiten Schlingen durch das Altmühltal mäandern – Deutschlands größten Naturpark.

Bavaria – a land of castles

The famous Eichstaetter Garden was built in the second half of the 16th century, surrounding the Willibaldsburg (Castle of Willibald) in Eichstatt (top), on the Altmuehl River. A stroke of luck: The Harburg (right), situated between Noerdlingen and Donauwoerth, narrowly escaped destruction in 1800 when its Austrian defenders surrendered to French troops, who were threatening to blow up the packed munitions depot.

Burgenland Bayern

Rund um die Willibaldsburg in Eichstätt (oben) an der Altmühl entstand in der zweiten Hälfte des 16. Jahrhunderts der berühmte Eichstätter Garten.
Ein Glücksfall anderer Art: Die Harburg (rechts), zwischen Nördlingen und Donauwörth gelegen, erlebte 1800 eine dramatische Rettung in allerletzter Minute; österreichische Verteidiger ergaben sich den Franzosen, die schon die Lunten an die randvolle Munitionskammer legen wollten.

Auferstanden aus Ruinen

Nur wenige deutsche Großstädte umschließen
einen so attraktiven, mittelalterlich gepräg-
ten Stadtkern wie Bayerns zweitgrößte Stadt
Nürnberg. Trotz schwerer Bombardements
im Zweiten Weltkrieg konnte die ehemalige
Reichsstadt viel von ihrem alten Glanz retten
beziehungsweise wieder aufpolieren.

Rising from the ruins

Very few large German cities still have as
attractive a medieval centre as does Nuernberg, Bavaria's second largest city. In spite
of heavy bombardment during the Second
World War, this former imperial city was able
to salvage, or at least restore, much of its
earlier lustre.

Im Zeichen der Burg

Die Kaiserburg, deren Baubeginn in die Regierungszeit von Heinrich III. (11. Jahrhundert) fällt, ist zweifellos das optische Zentrum Nürnbergs. Heute ist die Frankenmetropole berühmt für ihre Bratwürste, ihre Lebkuchen und ihre Spielzeugindustrie.

In the sign of the castle

The Kaiserburg, whose construction began during the reign of Emperor Heinrich III (11th century), is unquestionably the visual centerpiece of Nuernberg. Today, this Franconian metropolis is known for its Bratwurst, Lebkuchen (a type of spiced biscuit), and toy industry.

FOLLOWING SPREAD

Let there be light

In the fog and darkness of the heart, faith can give one direction and stability. This conviction was set into stone in Bavaria more than in virtually any other Christian land in the world. As can be seen in this chapel near Neumarkt, only the very best master-builders, stucco artists, and painters were selected to give physical form to the worship of God.

FOLGENDE DOPPELSEITE

Der Herr ist die Klarheit

Im Nebel und in der Finsternis des Herzens gab der Glaube Richtung und Halt. Diese Überzeugung wurde in kaum einer anderen christlichen Weltgegend so häufig in Stein gesetzt wie in Bayern. Und wie für diese Kapelle bei Neumarkt fanden sich stets die besten Baumeister, Stuckateure und Maler, um das Lob Gottes zu gestalten.

Franken ist »Auch-Bayern«

Es ist nicht ganz einfach – und schon gar nicht mit einem Wort – zu sagen, was »Franken« bedeutet. Wer das nördliche Bundesland Bayern meint und Irrtümer vermeiden will (das Wort »Franken« bezeichnet ja auch die Gesamtheit der unter Karl dem Großen zwangsvereinigten west- und mitteleuropäischen Stämme), spricht am besten von »Mainfranken«. Das wäre dann der Landschaftsraum am mittleren und oberen Main, an Kocher und Jagst, etwa die Regierungsbezirke Ober-, Mittel- und Unterfranken (in Bayern) sowie der Regionalverband Franken in Baden-Württemberg.

Franken sind »Auch-Bayern«. In halb ironischer, halb durchaus ernst gemeinter Attitüde wehren sie sich dagegen, als Bayern vereinnahmt zu werden. Man ist Franke (gesprochen: »Fronge«) und gehört zum Bundesland Bayern. Die image-bestimmenden Oberbayern mit ihrem – im Wortsinne – hervorragenden Alpensaum nennt der Franke ganz gern »Nordtiroler«.

Der Main (links eine Morgenimpression) ist mit seinen 574 Kilometern Gesamtlänge zwar nur ein Nebenfluss des Rheins, seine Bedeutung als kulturelle Ader und über die Jahrhunderte als Befruchter von Handel und Wandel lässt ihn durchaus gleichauf mit Elbe und Donau strömen.

Erdgeschichtlich gesehen ist es eher ein folgenreicher Zufall, dass aus dem Bach, der noch im Tertiär der Donau zufloss, ein Fluss wurde, der sich in Ost/West-Richtung durchschlängelt und dabei mehrere natürliche steinerne Sperren durchbrechen muss: Keuper- und Muschelkalk-Auftürmungen zum Beispiel.

Der Rhein-Main-Donau-Kanal, der die freie Durchfahrt vom Schwarzen Meer zur Nordsee ermöglicht, machte den Main zu einer internationalen Transitstraße. Dem Namen nach. Denn das R-M-D-Projekt erbrachte nicht die Frachtraten, die sich Franken und Bayern von dem Großprojekt versprachen.

Franconia or »Also-Bavaria«

It is not easy, and certainly not in one word, to explain what »Franken« (Franconia) means. If you are talking about the northernmost part of Bavaria and want to avoid error (the word »Franken« also refers to all the tribes of west- and middle-European peoples who were forcibly unified under Charlemagne), you would be well-advised to speak of »Mainfranken«. This includes the areas around the middle and upper parts of the Main, Kocher, and Jagst Rivers – roughly encompassing the administrative districts of Upper, Middle, and Lower Franconia (in Bavaria), as well as the regional federation of Franconia in Baden-Wuerttemberg.

Franconians are »Also-Bavarians«. With a half-ironic yet half-serious attitude, Franconians vehemently protest at being called Bavarians. Instead, one is a »Franke« (pronounced »Frong-ge«), who lives in the province of Bavaria. Upper Bavarians who, with their enormous mountain landscapes, tend to colour the public image of the entire province, like to call Franconians »North Tyrolians«.

At 574 kilometers, the Main River (at left, in the morning) is only a tributary of the Rhine, but its meaning as a cultural artery and as a catalyst of trade and change over the centuries puts it in the same category of importance as the Elbe and Danube.

From a geological point-of-view, it is a coincidence rich with consequence that the stream, which once flowed into a tertiary of the Danube, grew into a river that winds from East to West. In the process it had to break its way through several natural stone barriers including, for example, vast accumulations of keuper and mussel limestone.

The Rhine-Main-Danube Canal, which allows free passage from the Black Sea to the North Sea, makes the Main into an international transit way, at least nominally. Unfortunately, the R-M-D Project did not produce the freight rates that Franconia and Bavaria expected.

A famous detour

Fortunately, the beautiful bends in the Main River at Volkach did not fall prey to the mania of hydraulic engineers for straight lines and forced short-cuts. Here, the Main is allowed to wind its phlegmatic way through small, local farmlands. The brown areas that appear to be lying fallow are actually fields full of one of the region's showpiece vegetables: asparagus.

Berühmte Schlenker

Die Mainschleifen bei Volkach wurden zum Glück keine Opfer wasserbaulicher Regelwut und zwanghafter Abkürzungsmanie. Behäbig kringelt sich der Main durch kleinräumige Ackerlandschaften. Die scheinbar brachen Braunflächen tragen ein Vorzeigegemüse der Region: Spargel.

The canal that had to be

According to its detractors, the Rhine-Main-Danube
Canal has »about as much sense as the Tower of Babel«.
Its construction was forced through in spite of massive
opposition by conservationists. Given that it is extremely
under-used today, its critics feel justified. The cloverleaf of
the Autobahn at Bibelsried, on the other hand, is a major
traffic distributor.

FOLLOWING SPREAD
Metaphors of light and steam

The rain-saturated cumulous clouds above the Steigerwald forest near Castell create a mood that combines both
gloom and hope shining through. Romantic painters sought
out natural formations of this kind whenever they wanted
to turn the sky into a giant backdrop for the pouring out
of their souls.

Der Kanal, der sein musste

Der Rhein-Main-Donau-Kanal galt unter Gegnern als »so
sinnvoll wie der Turmbau zu Babel« und wurde gegen den
großen Widerstand der Naturschützer durchgesetzt. Mit
Blick auf die mangelhafte Auslastung fühlen sich die Kritiker
heute bestätigt. Das Bibelrieder Autobahndreieck dagegen
ist ein echter Verkehrsverteiler.

FOLGENDE DOPPELSEITE
Metaphern aus Licht und Dampf

Die regensatten Haufenwolken über dem Steigerwald bei
Castell verbreiten eine Stimmung von Düsternis und durch-
scheinender Hoffnung: Formationen dieser Art suchten
romantische Maler, wenn sie den Himmel zur großen Kulisse
für ihre Seelenergießungen machen wollten.

Ein Strahl aus Gottes Fenster

So beschrieben empfindsame Gemüter
die Stimmung, die entsteht, wenn durch eine
Wolkendecke punktgestrahlt Licht auf eine
abgedunkelte Landschaft fällt. Hier stanzt die
Sonne bei Iphofen am Fuß des Steigerwaldes
ein Stück Maintal aus dem Halbschatten.

A ray of light from God's window

This is how sensitive souls describe the mood
that is created when a thin ray of light shines
through a heavy blanket of clouds, striking
a small area in an otherwise darkened landscape. Here you can see the sun highlight a
piece of the Main Valley, near Iphofen at the
foot of the Steigerwald forest.

A climate fit for a king

Aschaffenburg already developed into an important port
and place of trade on the right bank of the Main River in the
early Middle Ages. The stately Renaissance castle Johannisburg (built 1605–14) became the second residence of the
bishops of Mainz. The Bavarian King Ludwig I also loved this
town on the Main, because of its agreeable climate.

Klima für Könige

Am rechten Ufer des Mains gelegen, entwickelte sich
Aschaffenburg schon im frühen Mittelalter zu einem wichtigen
Hafen und Handelsplatz. Das stattliche Renaissanceschloss
Johannisburg (erbaut 1605–14) diente den Mainzer Bischö-
fen als Zweitresidenz. Auch Bayernkönig Ludwig I. liebte die
Stadt am Main – wegen ihres milden Klimas.

Rothenburg – nowhere more romantic

Whenever Germany wants to make a good impression abroad by emphasizing its cultural riches, a postcard view of Rothenburg ob der Tauber always does the trick. On certain days, you will find more Japanese and Americans than Germans in its cobblestone alleyways. After all, where else can you find so much medieval flair in one spot?

Rothenburg – mehr Romantik geht nicht

Immer wenn Deutschland im Ausland eine gute Figur machen will und seinen kulturellen Reichtum ins rechte Bild setzen will, geschieht das mit einer Postkartenansicht von Rothenburg ob der Tauber. Es gibt Tage, an denen hier mehr Japaner und Amerikaner als Deutsche die kopfsteinbepflasterten Gässchen füllen. Aber es stimmt ja: Wo sonst gibt's so viel mittelalterliches Flair auf einem Fleck?

Stadt des Klerus und der Bürger

Würzburg, Hauptstadt des Regierungsbezirkes Unterfranken, ist wesentlich älter als seine Baudenkmäler, die durch die verheerenden Bombardements im Zweiten Weltkrieg reduziert wurden. Ab dem 7. Jahrhundert existierte auf dem Marienberg eine Burg fränkischer Herzöge, das Castellum Wirciburg, das 704 erstmals urkundlich bezeugt wird. 741/42 gründet Bonifatius hier das Bistum Würzburg.

Erneut geschichtsnotorisch wurde Würzburg rund vierhundert Jahre später unter den Staufern. Deren berühmtester, Friedrich Barbarossa, feierte in den Mauern der Stadt 1156 seine Hochzeit; und in der Folgezeit wurden in der Mainmetropole regelmäßig Reichstage abgehalten – glanzvolle Versammlungen der gehobenen Stände, die den obersten Herrscher, König oder Kaiser, beraten sollten.

Ins Interesse der Geschichtsbücher rückt Würzburg vor allem dann, wenn es um klerikale Macht geht: Fürstbischöfe – also Geistliche mit weltlicher Macht – konnten sich hier stärker und länger festsetzen als in anderen deutschen Landesteilen. Was naturgemäß nicht allen gefiel. Würzburgs wirtschaftlich erstarkende Bürgerschaft entwickelte sich über die Jahrhunderte zum natürlichen Feind einer Herrscherschicht, die an Aufbruch und Fortschritt nicht sonderlich interessiert war.

Aber es waren nicht eigentlich die reichen Bürger, sondern die Bauern, deren 1525 blutig niedergeschlagener Aufstand die bis dato festgefügte Kirchenmacht schwächte. Schwächte – nicht abrupt aushebelte. Erst 1801 beendete die Säkularisation auch formal die fürstbischöfliche Regentschaft; 1803 kam Würzburg zu Bayern, wo es, von kurzen Unterbrechungen abgesehen, auch blieb.

Wer heute die Stadt und die Region besucht, kommt meist wegen der imposanten Burg auf dem Marienberg. Oder wegen der Werke des bedeutendsten deutschen Bildhauers und Bildschnitzers des 16. Jahrhunderts, Tilman Riemenschneider. Von dem Genie, das für seine Parteinahme zugunsten der rebellischen Bauern eingekerkert und gefoltert wurde, finden sich einige Hauptwerke, zum Beispiel im romanischen Dom, im Mainfränkischen Museum und im Umland.

City of clergy and burghers

Wuerzburg, capital city of the administrative district of Lower Franconia, is considerably older than its historical buildings, which were heavily reduced during the devastating bombings of the Second World War. Ever since the 7th century, a castle of Franconian dukes existed on the Marienberg. Castellum Wirciburg, as it was called, was first documented in 704 A. D. In 741/42 A. D. St. Boniface founded the bishopric of Wuerzburg here.

Wuerzburg became historically notable again approximately 400 years later under the Staufer dynasty. The most famous within this dynasty, Friedrich Barbarossa, celebrated his wedding within the walls of the city in 1156 A. D., and in the years following, Imperial Diets were regularly held in this metropolis on the Main – glittering assemblies of the highest estates of the realm, who were here to advise the most powerful ruler, king or emperor.

Above all, Wuerzburg comes to occupy an interesting position in history books when clerical power is involved. Prince-bishops, that is, clergymen who also wielded worldly power, were able to establish themselves here more firmly and for a longer time than in any other German land within the Holy Roman Empire. Of course, not everyone was happy about this. The middle class of Wuerzburg grew much stronger economically over the centuries, and developed into the natural enemy of a ruling class that was not particularly interested in fundamental change or progress.

However, somewhat surprisingly, it was not the wealthy burghers but the farmers who, although brutally crushed in their rebellion of 1525, ultimately weakened the power of the church that had been so entrenched until then. Weakened – but not overthrown. It was only in 1801 that secularization finally put a formal end to the rule of the prince-bishops. Shortly thereafter, in 1803, Wuerzburg joined Bavaria, where it remained – with a few brief interruptions.

People who visit the city and the region today come mostly to see either the imposing castle on top of the Marienberg or the work of Tilman Riemenschneider, the most significant wood carver of the 16th century. Several of this genius' masterpieces (he was imprisoned and tortured for siding with the rebellious farmers) can be found in Wuerzburg's Romanesque cathedral, in the Mainfrankisches Museum, and in the surrounding area.

Klein-Versailles hoch überm Main

Versailles war für viele Baumeistergenerationen das Maß aller Dinge, wenn es um repräsentative Großbauten ging. Ob der berühmteste deutsche Baumeister seiner Zeit, Balthasar Neumann, auftragsgemäß oder freiwillig nach Paris geschielt hat, als er die Würzburger Bischofsresidenz plante und baute (1744 fertig gestellt), ist nicht ganz geklärt. Der Atheist Napoleon jedenfalls witzelte, das Bauwerk sei »Europas größter Pfarrhof«.

Mini-Versailles high above the Main River

For many generations of architects, Versailles was the measure of all things related to large-scale building projects. But it is not known whether Balthasar Neumann, the most famous German architect of his time, went to Paris as part of his commission or voluntarily, after he was chosen to plan and build the residence of the Bishop of Wuerzburg. Napoleon, atheist that he was, used to joke that the complex was »Europe's biggest rectory«.

Der Atem der Jahrtausende

Die Festung Marienberg überragt Würzburg. Der Ort gäbe – wenn dafür nicht schriftliche Geburtsurkunden erforderlich wären – den 125 000 Einwohnern der Stadt die Legitimation, sich dreitausendjährig zu nennen: Spätestens im 8. Jahrhundert, vielleicht sogar 1000 vor Christus, gab es hier eine erste befestigte Siedlung. Um 500 v. Chr. hatten keltische Stammesführer ihren Sitz auf dem Marienberg.

The breath of millennia

The fortress of Marienberg towers over Wuerzburg. If written birth certificates were not a requirement, this place alone would give the 125,000 citizens of the city reason to declare themselves three-thousand years old. The first fortified settlement already existed here by the 8th century at the very latest, but possibly as far back as 1,000 B.C. Celtic tribal leaders had their seat on the Marienberg around 500 B.C.

Rhapsody in gold

Elements of relief usually lend a landscape its contours – mountains, hills, knolls, and so on. The landscape around Bad Neustadt on the Saale River in Franconia is comparatively unspectacular, unless the sky applies golden highlights.

Rhapsodie in Gelb

Meist ist es das Relief – Berge, Hügel, Kuppen – das einer Landschaft Kontur verleiht. Die Landschaft um Bad Neustadt an der Fränkischen Saale ist vergleichsweise unspektakulär – wenn nicht gerade der Himmel Glanzpunkte setzt.

»Art reduces life to its essentials«

This ancient tenet can be found in many treatises on aesthetics. It is also true for photographic art: less can be more. Anyone with a camera can manage to take a decent photograph if the scene is luxurious enough. But only a true photographer can successfully capture on film that which is both cool and reserved.

»Kunst ist die Reduktion auf das Wesentliche«

So laut ein alter Lehrsatz, der in fast jedem Buch über Kunst steht. Auch für die Fotokunst gilt: Weglassen kann bereichern. Üppige Motive erkennt jeder Foto-Handwerker. Um aber das Spröde ins Bild zu setzen, braucht es einen Lichtbildner.

Wohnen im Wehrschloss

Wasserschlösser wie dieses gut erhaltene Exemplar der Freiherrn von Bibra in Irmelshausen im nördlichen Unterfranken waren meist absichtsvoll in Stein gesetzte Kompromisse: Sie sollten möglichst gut vor Angriffen schützen und trotzdem hohen Wohnkomfort bieten.

Life in a military castle

Castles with moats, such as this well-preserved specimen belonging to the Baron of Bibra in Irmelshausen in the northern part of Lower Franconia, were mostly deliberate compromises set into stone. They were intended to provide the best possible protection from attacks, while still offering a high level of privacy and luxury.

Vorsicht mit Vergleichen …

… aber Bamberg provoziert sie: Es ist wie Rom auf sieben Hügel erbaut, wie Venedig von Wasserläufen durchzogen, und seine Altstadt ist so schön wie die von Prag. So jubeln nicht nur die Reiseführer. Auch die UNESCO zeigte sich beeindruckt und erklärte den Stadtkern 1993 zum Weltkulturerbe.

Die oberfränkische Stadt liegt im breiten Tal der Regnitz und lockt Touristen aus aller Welt mit einer eindrucksvollen Konzentration sakraler und profaner Bauwerke. Bambergs erste geschichtliche Erwähnung geschah 902 in Zusammenhang mit dem Fürstengeschlecht der Babenberger, die ebendort eine Burg hatten, wo heute der Bamberger Dom steht.

Die einschlägigen Architekturführer feiern diesen Dom als »ein Hauptdenkmal der spätromanisch-frühgotischen Kunst« – ein Monument des Übergangs. Am nördlichen Chorpfeiler befindet sich der ohne Zweifel berühmteste Repräsentant der Stadt, der »Bamberger Reiter«. Nicht nur sein hoheitliche Wesen, das sich in der Figur vergegenständlicht, auch das fortdauernde Rätselraten, wer hier eigentlich dargestellt wurde, machte die Plastik zu einem der berühmtesten Reiterstandbilder der Kunstgeschichte.

Kaum weniger wichtig für die Bekanntheit der Stadt über Landesgrenzen hinaus: Die Bamberger Symphoniker, 1946 als Nachfolgeorchester des Deutschen Opernhauses in Prag, der Prager Philharmonie und des Kurorchesters Karlsbad gegründet, sind ein Klangkörper von Weltruf.

Beware of comparisons …

… although Bamberg cannot help but provoke them. Like Rome, it is built on seven hills; like Venice, it is interwoven with waterways; and its historical center is as beautiful as that of Prague. Travel guides are not the only ones to trumpet their enthusiasm. UNESCO was also impressed enough to declare the city center a world cultural treasure.

This Upper Franconian town is situated in the wide Regnitz Valley and attracts tourists from all over the world with its impressive concentration of both religious and secular buildings. Bamberg first merited historical mention in 902 A.D., in connection with the princely house of the Babenbergers, who had a castle on the place where Bamberg Cathedral stands today.

Architectural guides celebrate this cathedral as »one of the most important monuments of late Romanesque/early Gothic architecture« – a monument of stylistic transition. On the northernmost pillar of the chancel you will find what is without question the most famous representative of the town: the so-called »Bamberg Rider«. Not only his majestic demeanor, which is embodied in the figure, but also the continuing riddle as to who he actually represents, makes this sculpture one of the most famous equestrian statues in art history.

Of no less importance to the town's reputation beyond Bavarian borders is the world class Bamberg Symphony. It was founded in 1946 as the orchestral successor to the German Opera House in Prague, which itself was created from the Prague Philharmonic and the Orchestra of the spa town of Karlsbad.

Banz Monastery near Bamberg

Kloster Banz in der Nähe von Bamberg

The crown of Franconia

The fortress of Coburg adorns itself with the additional title,
»The Crown of Franconia«. This name is justified not only
by its silhouette, but also by the riches the fortress contains:
some of the very best German paintings (for example, works
by Cranach, Duerer, and Gruenewald); the Luther Room;
the only two remaining Baroque coaches that are still in
working order; Venetian glass treasures; a historical weapons
collection, etc., etc., etc.

Die Krone Frankens

Die Feste Coburg schmückt sich auch mit dem Zunamen
»Die fränkische Krone«. Nicht nur ihr Umriss rechtfertigt
den Namen, mehr noch der Inhalt: deutsche Malerei vom
Feinsten (Cranach, Dürer, Grünewald), das Lutherzimmer, die
einzigen zwei noch fahrtüchtigen Barockkutschen, vene-
zianische Glaskostbarkeiten, eine historische Waffensamm-
lung etc. etc. etc.

Napoleon's reserve

The most famous visitor to the fortress of Kronach was, without doubt, Napoleon Bonaparte. Just before he launched his campaign against Prussia in the year 1806, Napoleon inspected the fortress on October 8th to determine if his forces would be able to occupy and defend it in case of a quick retreat. He threatened the Bavarian officers in charge of Kronach with the loss of their heads if they surrendered the castle to »the third assault«.

Napoleons Reserve

Der berühmteste Besucher der Feste Kronach war ohne Zweifel Napoleon Bonaparte. Vor Beginn seines Zuges gegen die Preußen im Jahre 1806 inspizierte er am 8. Oktober die Fest unter dem Aspekt, ob sich die Anlage im Falle eines raschen Rückzugs beziehen und verteidigen ließe. Er drohte den bayerischen Besatzungsoffizieren auf der Burg den Verlust ihrer Köpfe an, falls sie die Anlage »vor dem dritten Sturme« übergeben sollten.

Zwei Türme, zwei Baumeister

Die Wallfahrtskirche Vierzehnheiligen ober-
halb von Staffelstein könnte auch als Symbol
des guten Kompromisses gelten. Als Mitte des
18. Jahrhunderts der Ausbau der Kapelle zu
einer repräsentativen Basilika anstand, lagen
die Entwürfe zweier berühmter Architekten
vor, der von Gottfried Heinrich Krohne und der
von Balthasar Neumann. Krohne bekam die
Bauleitung, musste aber den Bauplan seines
Konkurrenten verwirklichen. Wie der Name
sagt, ist die Kirche den vierzehn »Nothelfern«
gewidmet – jenen Heiligen, die Gläubige in
verschiedenen Notlagen anrufen können.

Two towers, two architects

The pilgrimage church of Vierzehnheiligen,
just above Staffelstein, is a lasting symbol of
one of architectural history's good compromises. When the expansion of the original chapel into an impressive basilica was planned
in the middle of the 18th century, the designs
of two famous architects, Gottfried Heinrich
Krohne and Balthasar Neumann, were under
consideration. Krohne ultimately got the commission, but had to build according to the
design of his competitor. As its name suggests,
the church is dedicated to the fourteen »auxi-
liary saints«, the saints that believers can
invoke in different states of need.

Ökologische Untiefen

Sanft schlängelt sich die Donau dahin –
auf den letzten 70 naturbelassenen Kilometern zwischen Straubing und Vilshofen. Doch
die Binnenschiffer schimpfen seit Jahren,
der Fluss sei nicht tief genug, vor allem bei
Trockenheit im Sommer. Staustufen müssten
gebaut werden. Umweltschützer fordern
den Erhalt des Biotops und einen »sanften
Ausbau« ohne Stufen. Noch wird darüber
sehr unsanft gestritten.

Ecological shallows

The Danube gently winds its way towards the
unspoiled landscape of its final 70 kilometers
between Straubing and Vilshofen. However,
inland shippers have been complaining for
years that the river is not deep enough, especially during the dry summer months, and they
asked for locks to be built. Conservationists,
on the other hand, demand that this unique
ecosystem be preserved, and they ask for only
»gentle development« with no locks. Today,
people continue to argue heatedly over this.

123

Mecca for Wagnerians

Richard Wagner himself laid the cornerstone of »his« opera-house, the Festspielhaus, in 1872. The architect Otto Brückwald constructed the building according to Wagner's ideas on the »green hill« north of Bayreuth. Every summer, Wagnerians from all over the world come to visit the famous Bayreuth festival.

Mekka der Wagnerianer

Richard Wagner selbst legte 1872 den Grundstein zu »seinem« Festspielhaus. Der Architekt Otto Brückwald verwirklichte das Gebäude nach Wagners Ideen auf einer Anhöhe nördlich von Bayreuth, dem »grünen Hügel«. Alljährlich pilgern Wagnerianer aus aller Welt im Sommer hierher, um den berühmten Festspielen beizuwohnen.

Triumph from beyond the grave

Between 1813 and 1815 – after Napoleon's sun had set
at the gates of Moscow – Europe freed itself from French
domination. This triumphal spirit also swept through Bavaria, where King Ludwig I reached deep into state coffers
and had the Befreiungshalle, or »Hall of Liberation«, built near
the junction of the Danube and the Altmuehl Rivers. Its design
is based on the grave of Theodorich in Ravenna, Italy.

Eine Grabmalskopie als Siegesmal

Nachdem Napoleons Stern spätestens vor Moskau ge-
sunken war, befreite sich Europa in den Jahren 1813 bis
1815 von französischer Vorherrschaft. Siegerlaune auch in
Bayern: König Ludwig I. griff tief in den Staatssäckel und
spendierte nahe dem Zusammenfluss von Donau und Altmühl eine Befreiungshalle, die dem Grabmal Theoderichs
in Ravenna nachempfunden wurde.

Dom und Rom und guter Ton

Dome wurden für die Ewigkeit gebaut. Und manchmal dauerte es auch eine kleine Ewigkeit, bis ein solches Werk zu Gottes Lob vollendet war. Die Regensburger begannen um das Jahr 1250 mit dem Bau, der sich fast dreihundert Jahre hinzog. 1525 wurde der Bau wegen Geldmangels eingestellt. Die beiden 105 Meter hohen Türme wurden erst in den Jahren 1859 bis 1869 dazugestellt. Diese 600jährige Verspätung ändert nichts am Urteil der Fachwelt: Der Regensburger Dom ist das bedeutendste gotische Bauwerk Bayerns.

Die Regensburger Domspatzen, ein Knaben- und Männerchor von Weltruf, stellen gewissermaßen die lebende Verbindung zu den Ursprüngen der Stadt dar. Schon im 7. Jahrhundert soll es in Regensburg eine Sängerschule gegeben haben, die im 19. Jahrhundert mit großem Erfolg wiederbelebt wurde.

Die Patrizierhäuser und Geschlechtertürme aus dem 13. und 14. Jahrhundert geben Regensburg ein mittelitalienisches Flair. Sie sind die steinernen Zeugen eines lang anhaltenden Wohlstandes: So vielstöckig (bis zu zwölf Geschosse) baute man zu Beginn der Neuzeit nur, wenn man deutlich mehr als nur die nötigen Mittel hatte.

Sacred Sparrows

Cathedrals are built to last for eternity. And sometimes it takes a small eternity for one of these buildings erected for the glory of God to be completed. The citizens of Regensburg began to build their cathedral in 1250 A.D., a project that took almost 300 years to finish. In 1525 A.D. construction was temporarily halted because of a lack of funds. The two towers (measuring 105 meters each) were finally added between the years of 1859 and 1869. However, this 600 year delay did not change the judgment of the experts: that Regensburg Cathedral is the most significant Gothic edifice in all of Bavaria.

The »Regensburger Domspatzen« (»Domspatzen« means »cathedral sparrows«), a male choir of international renown, constitutes a living connection to the origins of the town. It is said that a choir school already existed in Regensburg as far back as the 7th century, which was later revived in the 19th century with tremendous success.

The patrician houses and dynastic towers of the 13th and 14th centuries still give Regensburg a medieval flair. They are the stone witnesses of a long-lived prosperity: at the beginning of modern times one could only build so high (as many as twelve storeys in some cases) if one had considerable funds.

To the eternal glory of the famous

Leo von Klenze, the court architect of King Ludwig I, built this marble culture clash of German and Greek in Donaustauf near Regensburg between 1830 and 1842. The Walhalla functions exclusively as a temple of glory, housing 121 marble busts of famous Germans.

Bad weather is relative

Frequent cloud gatherings just before the rise of the Bavarian Forest (left) grace the region with up to 2,000 millimeters of precipitation each year – a reliable supply for reservoirs of natural drinking water.

Zum Ruhme der Berühmten

Den germanisch-griechischen Culture-Clash aus Marmor erbaute Leo von Klenze, der Hofarchitekt König Ludwigs I., zwischen 1830 und 1842 in Donaustauf nahe Regensburg. In ihrer einzigen Funktion als Ruhmestempel beheimatet die Walhalla 121 Marmorbüsten berühmter Deutscher.

Schlechtes Wetter ist relativ

Häufiger Wolkenstau vor den Höhenlagen des Bayerischen Waldes (links) beschert der Region mit bis zu 2000 Millimeter mittlerer Niederschlagsmenge pro Jahr zuverlässigen Nachschub für die natürlichen Trinkwasserreservoirs.

Die heilige Drei

Die Wallfahrtskirche zur Heiligen Dreifaltig-
keit bei Waldsassen verbildlicht mehrfach die
Idee der dreieinigen Gottheit: Vater, Sohn und
Heiliger Geist. Den 1685 bis 1689 errichteten
Rundbau überragen drei große und drei kleine
Türme. Der Sakralbau umfasst drei Rundchöre,
drei Seitenkapellen und drei Altäre. Der Ge-
stalter, der barocke Baumeister Georg Dietzenhofer, war gelernter Maurermeister: Vielleicht
hätte ein studierter, zünftiger Architekt nicht
den Mut gehabt, die übliche Formsprache
seiner Zeit so radikal zu ignorieren.

The Holy Number Three

The pilgrimage church of the Heilige Dreifal-
tigkeit (Holy Trinity) at Waldsassen repeatedly
embodies the idea of the divine Trinity: God
the Father, Son, and Holy Spirit. Three large
and three smaller towers loom over the
rotunda, built between 1685 and 1689. The
main church building is comprised of three
round choirs, three side chapels, and three
altars. Georg Dietzenhofer, the Baroque builder
who designed the church, was a master
mason by trade. A trained expert architect
probably would not have had the courage
to ignore the formal architectural language
of his era in such a radical manner. **131**

The Bavarian Forest   Der Bayerische Wald

Gestautes Regen-Wasser

Mit 86 Metern Höhe und 640 Metern Länge ist die Tal-
sperre Frauenau eine der größten Stauanlagen Deutschlands.
Das riesige Reservoir wird gespeist vom »Kleinen Regen«,
einem Quellflüsschen des Donau-Nebenflusses Regen.
Schon bevor hier seit 1980 glasklares Trinkwasser gesammelt
wurde, war diese Ecke des Bayerischen Waldes berühmt
für ihre Glasproduktion.

Capturing rainwater

At 86 meters high and 640 meters long, the Frauenau
dam complex is one of the largest hydraulic facilities in Germany. Its enormous reservoir is fed by the »Little Regen«,
an offshoot of the Regen River, which is itself a tributary
of the Danube. This neck of the Bavarian woods was already
famous for its glass industry, long before the reservoir began
to gather crystal clear water here in 1980.

Wasser im Keller, Geld im Sack

Wasserfarbspiele: Wo sich (von oben nach unten) Ilz, Donau und Inn vereinigen, im hochwassergefährdeten Passau, nahmen die Einwohner seit alters her nasse Füße und Schlimmeres in Kauf: Der Standortvorteil – die Schiffsverbindung nach Wien kreuzt den Haupthandelsweg nach Böhmen – machte regelmäßige Überschwemmungen verschmerzbar.

Water in the cellar, money in the bag

At the confluence of the (from top to bottom) Ilz, Danube, and Inn Rivers, the town of Passau rests on a flood plain.
Its citizens have always had to reckon with wet feet, and sometimes worse. Although Passau is advantageously located at the crossroads of the shipping route to Vienna and the main trade route to Bohemia, it also suffers regular and painful floods.

Jazzakkorde, Längenrekord

Burghausen an der Salzach ist fest verzeichnet im Atlas der Weltmusik: Hier findet alljährlich eines der renommiertesten Jazzfestivals Europas statt. Der schmucke Ort ist auch ein Muss für die Liebhaber alter Wehrbauten: Hier dehnt sich (obere Bildhälfte) über gut 1000 Meter die längste Burganlage Deutschlands.

Jazz chords and German records

Burghausen on the Salzach River is firmly inscribed in the Atlas of World Music. Every year, this is where one of Europe's most famous jazz festivals takes place. The pretty town is also a must-see for lovers of old military buildings, where Germany's biggest mountain military base (upper half of photograph) extends over a distance of at least 1000 meters.

Bayerns höchste Spitze

Bayerns und damit auch Deutschlands höchster Berg, die Zugspitze, verfehlt mit ihren 2962 Metern die Dreitausendermarke nur knapp. Der Gipfel ist fest einbetoniert und trägt Aussichtsplattform, Gastronomie, die Gipfelstation der Zahnradbahn, die vom Eibsee herauffährt, und eine meteorologische Station.

Die liegt abseits vom üblichen Rummel, der sich am höchsten Punkt der Republik beinahe rund ums Jahr entfaltet. In der reinen Hochgebirgsluft sind mit ultra-sensiblen Messinstrumenten noch Spurenelemente nachweisbar, die normalerweise vom »Umgebungsdreck« überlagert sind. Messungen bis in die Molekularstruktur hinein sind heute Stand der Wissenschaft. Und so ist es kein Zufall, dass Bayerns Spitzen-Messtechnologie auf der Zugspitze auf die Spitze getrieben wird.

Bavaria's highest peak

The Zugspitze, which is Bavaria's as well as Germany's highest mountain, falls just short of the three-thousand meter mark. The peak is practically embedded in concrete and supports viewing platforms; restaurants; the end station of the rack-railway that climbs the mountain from the waters of the Eibsee far below; and a meteorological station.

This meteorological station is situated away from the general hubbub that is heard almost year round on the highest peak of the republic. In the pure high mountain air, ultra-sensitive instruments make it possible to prove the presence of trace elements normally rendered undetectable by environmental pollution. Today, science is able to make very precise measurements, even of minute details of molecular structure. And so it is no accident that Bavaria's most sophisticated technology is carried to extremes on the Zugspitze.

Bayern in Zahlen / Some Facts for the Visitor

Bevölkerung / Population

Bayern ist in sieben Regierungsbezirke unterteilt, in denen insgesamt 12,4 Millionen Menschen leben, darunter 1,2 Millionen Ausländer.

Bavaria is divided into seven administrative districts. The total population of Bavaria is 12.4 million people, which includes 1.2 million foreigners.

Die Regierungsbezirke Administrative districts	Fläche in km² Area in km²	Bevölkerung Population
Oberbayern (München)	17 539	4 195 673
Niederbayern (Landshut)	10 329	1 194 472
Oberpfalz (Regensburg)	9 690	1 089 826
Oberfranken (Bayreuth)	7 230	1 109 674
Mittelfranken (Ansbach)	7 244	1 706 615
Unterfranken (Würzburg)	8 531	1 344 740
Schwaben (Augsburg)	9 992	1 782 386

Es gibt acht Großstädte mit 100 000 Einwohnern und mehr.

Bavaria has eight cities with a population of 100,000 inhabitants or more.

Die fünf größten Städte The five biggest cities	Einwohner Inhabitants
München	1 247 873
Nürnberg	493 553
Augsburg	259 217
Würzburg	132 687
Regensburg	128 604

Geografie / Geography

Die Fläche des Freistaates Bayern umfasst 70 555 Quadratkilometer. Die höchste Erhebung Bayerns (und zugleich Deutschlands) ist die Zugspitze, die niedrigste Stelle der Wasserspiegel des Mains bei Kahl am Main (100 Meter).

The Free State of Bavaria covers a total area of 70,555 square kilometers. The point of highest elevation in Bavaria (and simultaneously Germany) is the Zugspitze, and the lowest point of elevation is where the water of the Main River flows past Kahl am Main (100 meters above sea level).

Die fünf höchsten Berge The five highest mountains	Meter Height in meters
Zugspitze (Wettersteingebirge)	2 962
Watzmann (Berchtesgadener Alpen)	2 713
Mädelegabel (Allgäuer Hochalpen)	2 645
Dreitorspitz (Wettersteingebirge)	2 633
Alpspitze (Wettersteingebirge)	2 628

Südbayern besitzt zahlreiche Seen. Die meisten Alpenvorlandseen – wie Chiemsee, Starnberger See und Ammersee – entstanden als Zungenbecken eiszeitlicher Gletscher. Die eingebetteten Alpenseen – wie etwas der Walchensee – verdanken ihre Entstehung alpiner Gebirgsbildung.

Southern Bavaria has numerous lakes. Most of the lakes found in the landscape that stretches beyond the foothills of the Alps were carved out by glaciers during the last ice age. The lakes that are embedded in the mountains themselves – for example, the Walchensee – were formed at the same time that the mountains were created.

Die fünf größten Seen The five largest lakes	Fläche in km² Area in km²	Größte Tiefe in m Greatest depth in m
Chiemsee	79,9 km²	73,4
Starnberger See	56,35 km²	127,8
Ammersee	46,60 km²	81,1
Walchensee	16,11 km²	189,5
Forggensee (bei Normalstau)	15,11 km²	35,3

Wirtschaft / Economy

46 Prozent der Fläche Bayerns werden landwirtschaftlich genutzt, Bayern besitzt innerhalb Deutschlands die größte Anzahl an landwirtschaftlichen Betrieben (146 162).

46 per cent of Bavaria's land is used for agriculture. Bavaria has the largest number of agricultural businesses in all of Germany (146,162).

Zu den bedeutendsten Industriezweigen in Bayern zählen die elektrotechnische und Textilindustrie, der Maschinen- und Fahrzeugbau und die chemische Industrie. Dies spiegelt sich auch in den bayerischen Exportschlagern wider:

Electrical engineering, textiles, machine and vehicle manufacturing and the chemical industry are among Bavaria's most important industries. This is also reflected in statistics that show Bavaria's top exports:

Exportschlager	in Milliarden Euro
Personenkraftfahrzeuge und Wohnmobile	22,8
Fahrgestelle, Karosserien, Motoren, Teile und Zubehör	6,4
Geräte zur Elektrizitätserzeugung und -verteilung	5,2
Maschinen	3,8
Vollständige Fabrikationsanlagen	3,3

Top exports	in billions of Euros
Cars and motor homes	22.8
Chassis, car bodies, motor parts and accessories	6.3
Electrical generation and distribution equipment	5.2
Various machines	3.8
Complete manufacturing facilities	3.3

Tourismus / Tourism

Meistbesuchte Burgen und Schlösser Most popular Castles and Chateaus	Besucher (2003) Visitors (2003)
Schloss Neuschwanstein	1 147 803
Schloss Nymphenburg	555 477
Schloss Herrenchiemsee	479 063
Schloss Linderhof mit Parkbauten	461 620
Würzburg, Residenz	323 079
Befreiungshalle Kelheim	176 708

RECHTE SEITE

Die Trudbertkapelle bei Waltrams

The Trudbert Chapel near Waltrams

Bibliografische Information Der Deutschen Bibliothek
Die Deutsche Bibliothek verzeichnet diese Publikation in der Deutschen Nationalbibliografie;
detaillierte bibliografische Daten sind im Internet über http://dnb.ddb.de abrufbar.

Originalausgabe
Copyright © 2005 von dem Knesebeck GmbH & Co. Verlags KG, München
Ein Unternehmen der La Martinière Groupe

Alle Fotografien wurden von Gerhard Launer aufgenommen mit Ausnahme der folgenden:
S. 30 und S. 78: Tobias Launer
Gestaltung: Herneid von dem Knesebeck
Umschlaggestaltung: Fabian Arnet
Lektorat: Christina Kotte
Satz: satz & repro Grieb, München
Druck: Uhl, Radolfzell
Printed in Germany

ISBN 3-89660-260-8

www.knesebeck-verlag.de